CONCRETELOOP.COM PRESENTS:
ANGEL'S LAWS OF
BLOGGING

CONCRETELOOP.COM PRESENTS:

ANGEL'S LAWS OF BLOGGING

WHAT YOU NEED TO KNOW
IF YOU WANT TO HAVE A SUCCESSFUL
AND PROFITABLE BLOG

ANGEL LAWS WITH CAROLE MOORE

Skyhorse Publishing

Copyright © 2011 by Angel Laws and Carole Moore

All Rights Reserved. No part of this book may be reproduced in any manner without the express written consent of the publisher, except in the case of brief excerpts in critical reviews or articles. All inquiries should be addressed to Skyhorse Publishing, 307 West 36th Street, 11th Floor, New York, NY 10018.

Skyhorse Publishing books may be purchased in bulk at special discounts for sales promotion, corporate gifts, fund-raising, or educational purposes. Special editions can also be created to specifications. For details, contact the Special Sales Department, Skyhorse Publishing, 307 West 36th Street, 11th Floor, New York, NY 10018 or info@skyhorsepublishing.com.

www.skyhorsepublishing.com
Skyhorse® and Skyhorse Publishing® are registered trademarks of Skyhorse Publishing, Inc.®, a Delaware corporation.

10 9 8 7 6 5 4 3 2 1

Library of Congress Cataloging-in-Publication Data is available on file.
ISBN: 978-1-61608-268-0

Printed in China

For my parents Garry and Mamie Laws,
Thank you for cultivating my uniqueness as a child, supporting my creativity as
a teenager, and providing me with inspiration as a young adult.

Contents

The pre-Law:
Getting to Know Angel

Angel at work in her
office in New York City.

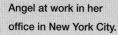

PHOTO: Felicia Mancini

In 2008, *Time* magazine recognized Concrete Loop as one of the fifty best websites on the Internet. This was a great honor, but an unusual one because at that time few website awards went to urban entertainment blogs, let alone one created by a young woman.

This recognition shed light on minority blogging and made advertisers wake up to the fact that blogging was indeed a business. As more and more bloggers start making real money doing this, our influence continues to expand and grow. I know because I make the majority of my income by blogging, and am bombarded with questions on a daily basis on how I came this far.

If anyone would have told me a couple of years ago I would be writing a book on this topic, I would have laughed it off. After all, when I started my blog, I was twenty years old, living with my parents, barely making it in college, and working a dead-end job. But I always believe that if you work hard at one thing long enough, you don't have anywhere to go but up. Even if that thing starts off as a hobby, as Concrete Loop did, you never know where it may lead.

During the early stages of Concrete Loop, one of my dreams was to be to black entertainment blogging what Oprah Winfrey was to afternoon talk shows. I still have a ways to go, but I can proudly say that Concrete Loop is one of the world's top black entertainment blogs, with millions of hits and a rock-hard reputation for positivity. And it doesn't get any better than that.

You're probably asking what this all has to do with you and your blogging dreams. Let me tell you what this book is going to do for you: It'll walk you along the same path I took, from buying my first domain to building Concrete Loop into the premiere, minority-owned and operated blog that it is today. Remember, blogging is for everyone and anyone can do it, no matter your choice of topic.

This book will also explain how I got to the top, clue you in on what you need to do to stay there, and give you a glimpse as to where I think blogging is headed in this highly competitive industry, with solid advice on how to set up and operate a celebrity- or entertainment-focused blog too, if that's where you want to focus.

So whether you want to blog for your bread and butter or simply stick a little extra dough in your wallet, blogging is your trip ticket. But like any journey, if you don't know where you're going or how to get there, you'll get lost, as well as waste a lot of money. I'm going to cut through all that information, give you what you need, then show you how to get there the right way. But first, let me tell you how I got to where I am. Maybe you can relate.

Getting to know Angel Laws

Before the celebs, the trips, and the swag came into my life, I was a military brat who grew up on bases all around the United States. My formative years had a significant influence on the person I am today.

Come to think of it, saying I'm a military brat is a bit of an understatement. I was even born on a military base: Camp Lejeune, which is in Jacksonville, on the coast of North Carolina. My father, Garry Laws, served in the United States Marine Corps for almost thirty years and we moved around a lot during my early years. I grew up in places like Florida, South Carolina, and Hawaii. In fact, South Carolina is where my dad first met my mother, Mamie. He was stationed at Parris Island as a young marine and she lived in the adjacent town, Beaufort. Dad was an only child from New York City and Mom came from a big, close, extended family. And as they say, the rest is history.

Besides old-fashioned family values, my parents also shared a strong commonality: They believed in the importance of a good education and working hard for what you want no matter the obstacle. My dad received his master's degree while he was still in the military and was going back and forth overseas on duty. He has always been a great role model for me, and now that he is a retired veteran turned middle school teacher, I see he is now a role model for others.

My mother, who is a registered nurse, received her degree while caring for my siblings and me. I have memories of my mom up late studying for a test, often getting only a couple of hours' sleep before she had to climb out of bed and go to work. Despite holding down a full-time job and having a family to take care of, she made good grades, and that always inspired me because she never complained about it.

I have three brothers, one older and two younger (twins), and they have also been a great inspiration for me. When I think back and reflect, my family has always been the driving force in helping me recognize my full potential.

As the only girl in the family, college played an important role when I started Concrete Loop, but not exactly in the way you might think. More about that in a minute; first, let me tell you how I prepared myself for a career as a web entrepreneur.

As a child, I was always finding innovative ways to make my own money. When I was eleven, my father was stationed in Kaneohe, Hawaii, and let's just say I started off as a loner and had a lot of time to come up with money- making plans. Sometime around sixth or seventh grade, I decided to go into business for myself. I priced candy at the base commissary, where it was not only cheaper, but didn't have any taxes added, and decided that I could buy there and resell it to the kids at school off base for a profit. I was making pretty decent money when the school got wind of it and told me I was prohibited from selling candy on school grounds. I didn't know it at the time, but this was the middle school version of what real-life entrepreneurs get thrown at them. You start doing well and then, boom! Like the commercial says, "Life comes at you." The difference between the ones who make it and the ones who don't really comes down to how you handle the curves business and life throw at you. I handled the ban on selling candy at school by moving my operation from the school buildings to the school buses. There wasn't any rule that prohibited selling candy on the bus, so I rolled with that punch and made a nice profit too.

That wasn't my only source of income either. Although I was barely in my teens, I was pretty computer savvy for the times. I have been into computers since my family first owned one of the old-school Apple computers with a dial-up modem. Remember that screechy sound they made when connecting and how it tied up the phone?

I didn't just get on the computer a lot—I took it apart and learned how it worked from the inside out. I cleaned it, explored it, and pretty much dominated it. If anyone in my family wanted to use the computer, they had to kick me off first because that's what I did with my spare time. I would work on the computer forever—sometimes as much as twelve hours at a stretch. (Actually, I haven't yet broken that habit.) My parents would even ground me for staying up late and sneaking on.

Although I was obviously obsessed with the computer, my first true love was actually creating computer graphics. Graphics were a natural offshoot of my two other obsessions: art and photography. My dad is a good photographer, and as a daddy's girl, I think I have always tried to emulate him. But I also developed some natural talent and an eye for color, form, and composition, which I spent years refining on the family computer.

One of the most popular sites when I was first cutting my teeth with computer graphics was www.Blackplanet.com, a social networking site where, like MySpace, you could make your own customized web page. None of the kids I knew really had a lot of experience in graphics and coding and I wasn't Leonardo da Vinci, but I knew what I was doing, and so I started supplementing my candy sale money by designing Blackplanet pages for classmates. For a little extra, I'd throw in a custom-designed graphic with whatever they wanted. I wasn't even old enough to drive, but I was already figuring out how to make money off the net.

That's not to say I think I'm the smartest or the most intuitive or even the most creative person to hit the Internet. Nope. I'm just saying that as with anything, you have to be able to see all of the possibilities if you're going to turn a profit. It's all about the vision and follow-through.

When I was a kid, I saw opportunities on two fronts to turn my talents into money: by becoming the middleman in my candy sales and developing marketable web skills. In both cases, I considered what I could do that was unique enough for people to pay for and whether the profit margin was great enough to justify the investment—both of money and time—on my part.

Understand that you can't always know that what you're doing is going to be hot. Sometimes it's just a matter of having the right idea at the right time. But good planning makes it less likely that you're wasting your time. It's like a fashion designer who makes a line of clothes with no particular clientele in mind. Maybe they'll catch on, maybe not; but if they're aimed at a hip-hop audience, high schoolers, or young career-minded women, the designer is able to know and understand the target market, giving the designer a better shot at success. My target clientele back when I was a kid was pretty simple. I targeted kids who like candy (which pretty much meant all of them) and people who wanted a better web presence. I knew the clients, and I knew how to meet their demands.

At school I continued my computer education by taking a computer class and found out that due to my Internet obsession, I knew more about it than the teacher did. In fact, I could have taught the class better than she did because I had more experience. I quickly became the go-to student for graphics and coding and often got sent to other teacher's classes to help with computer-related problems.

During this time, I became immersed in the world of personal domains. My Internet peers were creating their own websites (called online journals) where they would speak about what was going on in their lives. This was the early stages of blogging but it wasn't being called that back then. When I was thirteen, I begged my dad to purchase a domain for me (urbanbliss. org—don't ask me how I came up with that name) so I could take a crack at this new trend. Very quickly this started to consume my life and soon everything I did was geared towards my online journal. Little did I know that this was just another training ground for what I am currently doing with Concrete Loop.

As I approached high school, I was ready to start making more money, and it was at this point in my life that I got my first real job, bagging groceries at the base commissary in Hawaii.

The way it worked was we stood in a line, and when the next customer came up, we bagged their groceries. We weren't paid anything by the commissary; all we earned were tips. So if you got a really bad tipper, you were basically out of luck. I did pretty well bagging groceries because I knew how to talk to the customers and I didn't mind hard work. This job taught me a lot about dealing with people face-to-face, and it's a skill you're going to need, even with an Internet-based business. Remember that you want to always think about taking your business to the next level, which means networking. Having experience dealing with customers in any capacity is a plus you can put to good use down the road, so don't go thinking that job you took as a teen flipping burgers was a timewaster. Your time at the drive-through window can help amp up your future. Everything has a lesson to be learned.

Eventually, I was moved up the ranks to cashier, a job I got through a government school program for students with a GPA of 3.5 or higher. I was also sticking with my graphic design hobby, making customized T-shirts and stickers for friends, updating my online journals, and developing my art and graphics abilities by continuing to work on my technical computer skills. At that time, I was really impressed with a graphic artist named Huny Young, who was popular back in the early days of urban online journaling for her innovative websites. She was an inspiration, so I wrote and asked her how she achieved such fabulous results. It was from Young that I learned about Adobe Photoshop.

Finding Photoshop was like one of those cartoon moments when someone has an idea and a big lightbulb pops up overhead: It was a revelation. Although the program was expensive, they had great trial periods for it, so I downloaded a copy, took a picture of myself, and started playing with the application. Pretty soon I was making some cool graphics. Prior to that I was using a program called Paint Shop Pro, but Photoshop took the cake with some of their features.

By the time I graduated from high school in 2003, I was known for my computer skills and some of my teachers were recommending colleges and schools that they felt I should attend. I was also becoming a popular fixture in the urban online journal community, especially when it came to making graphics and customizing HTML.

After graduation, I enrolled in Hawaii Pacific University with the idea of becoming an art teacher. I was thinking major in art and minor in photography, a pretty decent mixture. I loved living in Hawaii and kept sharpening my skills while attending college. Grades were no problem, I was making excellent money as a cashier, and life was good. Then my dad got orders from the military to be transferred back to Camp Lejeune, North Carolina, where I was born. I had a choice of whether to go with the family or stay in Hawaii and complete my education. Since I spent almost eight years on the island of Oahu, I figured I was up for something new and decided to move with them. That decision changed my life, and ultimately led me to creating Concrete Loop.

After moving, I found out that my credits wouldn't transfer, so I couldn't get into the university I wanted to attend in North Carolina. As a result, I had to enroll in the local community college as a part-time student. After the move, I began to think I had made a big mistake. Not only was I in a new place, but all my friends were on the other side of the country. But as they say, everything happens for a reason.

By this stage of my life, I was very depressed and used all of my free time outside of class in creative pursuits. I would take self-portraits, paint, or create new websites. During that time, I was also holding down a job at the local Parks and Recreation Department where I did a lot of things, from working with the after-school program to supervising the skateboard park to reconciling the money from selling concessions. It was steady work, but uninspiring, and as soon as I got off, I headed for the family computer.

And as you know, getting on that computer was a battle. Up until then I had never owned my own computer and found that I had to share computer time with my three brothers. All of them wanted to check their e-mail, chat with their friends, and play games, meaning I had to fight for every minute of computer time yet again. When I wasn't working or taking pictures, I spent as much of my free time as possible on that computer, and while my family thought I was playing games or Internet surfing, what I was really doing was starting Concrete Loop.

Creating Concrete Loop

Here is how that went down. Back in November of 2005, I was already interested in popular and up-and-coming black entertainers. If I wanted to read about actors like Denzel Washington or Will Smith, I could find plenty about them through the power of message boards. But if I was interested in getting the latest info on singers like Monica or Mary J. Blige, there was no central place online for me to go to catch up on what was happening in their lives. Of course we had magazines to look at, like *Vibe* or *Honey*, but their websites weren't up to par at the time. So I decided I'd fix that and start my own blog on entertainment—and whatever else caught my eye—with no real goal other than to entertain myself and some of my friends.

I tried out different names and finally came up with Concrete Loop because I wanted my information to be solid like concrete—not just a bunch of unsubstantiated rumors, but something you could take to the bank—and I wanted to keep any readers I might have in the loop. I thought Concrete Loop sounded pretty good and asked my younger brother Justin what he thought. He was seventeen at the time and told me the name sounded "wack" and to find something else to name my blog. However, I trusted my instincts and bought the domain. I can't imagine where I'd be if I hadn't trusted my instincts.

Now that I had Concrete Loop registered, I created a layout and started putting material on it. At first I made a lot of mistakes, like using photographs without permission (I didn't understand copyright and public domain, which I get to later) and underestimating my site traffic. I was completely unprepared when my ISP contacted me and said I owed them thousands of dollars because I had exceeded my bandwidth. (More about that in a later chapter too.)

But I survived all of the drama and continued to prosper and grow as I taught myself how to blog, and how to blog well. The big turnaround for Concrete Loop came courtesy of one of the most beautiful and well-known women in the world, Iman, the supermodel and wife of rocker David Bowie.

I had a picture of Iman on Concrete Loop where she was at an event with a nice dress on but when you zoomed down on her feet, you could see the years of runway walking had taken their toll. I made a funny caption post about it and the next thing I knew, someone contacted me and said Iman had mentioned Concrete Loop on her MySpace blog. I thought it was a joke but checked, and there it was: This international personality and fashion legend said she was wearing closed-toe shoes at her next event, so Angel of Concrete Loop "wouldn't make fun of me."

I sat there in shock, while meanwhile my website traffic went off the charts. The next thing I knew, I was getting contacted by a bunch of celebrities and people behind the scenes in the entertainment world. All this happening before the site celebrated its one-year anniversary. Then a second huge thing boosted the site: Superstar Kanye West shouted out Concrete Loop in a song he was featured on. The 2007 song "Pro Nails" was on his mixtape and his rhyme was like, "Please no cameras, they gon have me on Concrete Loop in my pajamas." I think that solidified the site within the celebrity world because Kanye is a pop culture icon. Pretty soon even more celebrities started talking to me, telling me they had become fans of the site. Tyrese Gibson, the actor/singer, gave me a lot of exclusive content and a few pointers about the music labels. He told me I should work with them more when it came to giveaways and exclusives. (More about this in "Angel's Eighth Law.") That was great advice, because talking to and working with the labels helped to morph Concrete Loop into what it is now.

When you learn, teach

Fast-forwarding to now, I also learned how to monetize my blog (and this is what this book is ultimately all about, how to make money blogging about what you love), and did it well enough to buy my first home with the money I made from Concrete Loop. I had no blueprint to follow, only my own common sense and constant trial and error. Whenever I had a business issue I couldn't figure out on my own, I went to my parents or brothers and they would help me figure out my next move.

I believe that instead of just talking about it, you should be about it. In other words, to paraphrase that Nike saying, DO IT, DON'T JUST RUN YOUR MOUTH. Using that philosophy is how Concrete Loop got started and how it continues to grow, as a business, a vision, and a brand.

Even though the website is currently five years old, it is still growing. I have lots of plans for the future and many places I want to take it—and you can do the same thing for your blog. The Internet is like outer space, wide open and ready to be conquered. And the opportunities for minority bloggers, entertainment bloggers, and any upcoming bloggers who simply just want to make some money are endless. You just have to make up your mind that you'll work as hard as it takes and get your ducks in a row.

Unlike you, I had to line those ducks up on my own by trial and error. But you won't have to. This book is going to help you to cut through some of the mountains of stuff I had to learn myself and provide you with a clear and easy road map that will jump-start your career as a successful blogger.

If you take the tools I'm providing you with here, use your creativity to develop your own unique brand, and work your butt off, you will find success. Don't get ahead of yourself though. First things first; you have to find the right subject and angle for your blog. We'll start at the beginning by figuring out how to mold whatever you're passionate about into a profitable blog; my passion has clearly been entertainment, so I've included some special advice on how to dive into that pool and come up with a winner.

Before we start, answer this question for me: What would you write about *if there was no money in it?*

That answer will tell you a lot about the type of blog you really want and where you want to go in this business.

Now let's get started.

Grab a Subject and Angle It!

If you love a subject so much you would write about it even if no one paid you, then you're also passionate about it. Good for you. Passion for your topic will be evident in both your writing and presentation, key things for a successful blog.

But being passionate alone doesn't necessarily translate into being commercial. That's where I come in. Whether you're just starting out with a new idea or you have an active blog you want to take to the next level, I can help you find a happy balance between your passion and being a commercial success. The ideas in this chapter will guide you in honing and crafting your concept to make it the best—and most profitable—it can be in a blogosphere that's as crowded as Concrete Loop's 2010 anniversary party.

As for my blog, I chose black entertainment because that was what interested me. It still does and that should be a key component to picking your topic. As I said above, more than anything else, you must love and be completely into what you're writing about, or you won't succeed as a blogger. A passing interest, something that you think you like but haven't really researched well, or a trend you think will have commercial potential—even though you don't know or care much about it— both of these situations almost always guarantee failure. You might do well at first, but when your interests shift, it will show in your work. You need a sustainable idea for your blog—and it can be trendy, but it must be relevant to who you are as a blogger. Don't worry if you don't truly know what you want to blog about yet; there are lots of ways to find the subject that best suits you.

Looking at the thousands upon thousands of blogs out there, it's not unrealistic to ask if there are any new ideas left, anything that hasn't yet been covered. I'm here to tell you there is always room for a new twist on an old concept or idea. For proof, consider the popularity of Twitter: Whoever would have thought a site that restricts communication to 140 characters could be so successful? It is at heart a simple notion that is easily executed. And tweeting is now a worldwide obsession.

When Choosing a
Subject, Make Sure
You Know:

1. What makes you
   comfortable
2. Your style
3. What you can afford

Facebook is another example of an idea that was inspired by other networking sites, caught on, and snowballed into a huge success. The founders of both of these sites share the ability to latch onto something and make it their own. This is what you have to do if you want your blog to be a commercial success.

But back to the question of whether there are any fresh subjects out there. My answer is both yes and no. The field of entertainment is a good example. Sure, there are thousands of sites that cover entertainment, but there's only one that does it like Concrete Loop. Look at the news networks: ABC, CBS, CNN, Fox, MSNBC, NBC,—all cover national news and host national news shows. Yet each one is different in approach, perspective, philosophy, and personality. News isn't supposed to be slanted, but if you tune in to CNN and Fox, you'll find a world of difference in the way those particular two networks approach the same subjects. That difference carries forward to their websites. Online and off, they slant their approaches to the same subjects to fit their ideologies: CNN tends to angle its stories left wing and liberal, while Fox turns a story right wing and conservative. This is how they tackle identical material, put their imprint on it, and make it their own, and it's a tactic you, too, can take to make your approach to something that's tried and true appear fresh and different.

Turning our background and interests into a profit-making machine

When you buy clothes, you base your choices on several things: personal experience (you know what looks good on your body and feels right when you wear it); what's in style (you keep up with fashion and want your look to reflect current trends without making you look cartoonish); and what you can afford (face it: we'd all wear Manolos if we had the money, but for most of us, there are those little things called food and electricity that we have to have). Now apply those same principles to choosing a subject for your blog. Here are a few things to consider when trolling for a good topic:

1. Know what makes you comfortable: Think of this as your favorite old T-shirt or pair of jeans, a piece of clothing that fits you to perfection and always feels right. Then translate that feeling to your blogging. What are you good at? What makes your heart race? When you're surfing the net, what catches your eye, makes you stop and pay attention? Concrete Loop is 100 percent true to who and what I am. Like I said in the previous

chapter, I loved reading about stars who were off the mainstream radar, but couldn't find really good, consistent coverage on them and other performers I admired. Because I had a fundamental understanding of the artists and their business, focusing on black entertainers who were not getting the press coverage of a Beyoncé or Usher was important to me. Since I couldn't find what I wanted, I decided to create it myself. You can too. Just take stock of your personal experience and interests. What trips your trigger? Do you love books or movies or a particular sport? Is mommyhood your thing or do you enjoy profession-related subjects? Go with something that you love, a subject that fits you, and you will want to sit down at the keyboard every day and type.

2. Know your style: Just because fashion houses are saying boots and animal prints are in this season or that accessories must now be bold and chunky doesn't mean that's what you want to wear. You don't just want to wander around copying the current trends and the same is true when you choose your subject. You want a topic that's current, but with the classic goodness of one that fits your overall style. Of course it never hurts to incorporate a classic element—like a little black dress—but you want to make sure you put your own twist on it. In other words, you want to choose a subject that is not only hot, but has staying power.

3. Take video games as an example: Say you love a certain video game and build a blog around it. Then a new version comes out—dope! You can keep on blogging about it and focus on the update. But what if the manufacturer decides the game you love is a dud and doesn't continue to market new versions, so that interest in that game withers away to nothing? Where does that leave you? From where I'm sitting, it leaves you with a blog that is going to lose its readership as your followers find other games—and blogs—that cater to their interests. You need to make sure your subject is broad enough to have staying power and that that topic is adaptable and fluid. Rather than picking a video game, why not focus on a certain type or ones with a similar theme? That way, even if a particular game is canceled, you'll still have plenty of other material to blog about. Choosing black entertainment offered me the best of both worlds. Unlike a one-note subject, it's a field that changes—new faces come into the scene all of the time—yet the classic performers are still out there.

4. Know what you can afford: It's not just about what you can afford in money, but also what you can afford in time and knowledge. One reason many mommy bloggers do well is that they focus on something they know and the learning curve is small for them. Heck, many of them use their learning curve as impetus for blog material and capitalize on learning

their craft. I think that's pretty smart. But while picking up a new skill is admirable (I really believe life is all about stretching yourself), you may find you're better off without the hurdle of a steep learning curve. Do you have a day job (I did when I started blogging), and if so, how much time can you devote to researching your subject? Face it, even if you're an expert on a subject, there could be an enormous investment in time spent researching what you're writing about. And for some of you, researching a topic could mean spending some money.

If you want to write about specific products, you need to first ask yourself if these products are available to you for free, or if you'll have to pay for them. The plethora of product review sites has really lessened the ability of bloggers to obtain samples in many cases, particularly if you're writing about something high-end or expensive. If you want to write about travel or other experiences, remember that travel can be a very expensive undertaking. Can you really afford to do this? Even experienced travel writers often have difficulty finding comped rooms, flights, meals, etc. How will you handle costs such as these?

The upshot is when you are picking a topic for your blog, you need to decide if it's because you're passionate about it or you want to make some money off of it. If it's for the former, the sky's the limit. But if you're in it for both passion *and* money, you need to give more thought about both the feasibility and marketability of your topic. Approach it as if you're putting together a travel wardrobe and consider who you are, the places you will be going, and the people you will be meeting while wearing those clothes—only in your case instead of going somewhere, you're bringing advertisers and readers to you, and you need to make sure your blog is appealing to both groups.

Narrowing in on a subject

Here is a creative way to nail down a terrific topic: Sit down and make a list of the top five things that interest you. Give it some thought because one of those five could turn into a great blog topic—but combining two or more of those interests could make both a great blog topic and a unique one.

Say your list looks like this:

1. Couture fashion
2. Handsome guys
3. Sunny warm climates
4. Festivals
5. Gardening

How can you mash up some of these to come up with blog topics? Festivals in sunny warm climates; handsome guys who wear couture fashion (Usher in Dsquared comes to mind); handsome guys in sunny, warm climates; festivals built around horticulture (the town of Wilmington, just south of Jacksonville, has a big Azalea Festival every spring); handsome guys who garden? Mix and match your interests until you come up with a unique take that is completely you. And, while you're at it, you might just find a combination that no one else has put together. You can make your blog different and as much yours as your signature.

And there's nothing wrong with blogging about one primary subject (or a combination) and, as your blog grows, adding new ones. I started out blogging about celebrities, and now, among other things, I also blog about fashion, books, news, and, reflective of my military brat background, how Memorial Day is celebrated overseas. You don't have to focus on the add-ins, but you do have to know when and how to mix in other topics. Concrete Loop, for example, not only honors performers who have stood the test of time, but also black history. You can start with one premise or a blend of topics and then bring in others as you build your readership and get to know what interests them. The important thing to remember is that unless you're producing something the readers want to see, you might as well be journaling.

More about mixing and matching

Remember, you're providing the content, so it can read any way you want it to, but it won't make sense if you just randomly mix topics. Think about wearing a great outfit with the right accessories and shoes to match—the combination gives you a fashionable look. But what if, after you've achieved that perfect look, you put another pair of pants and a skirt on top of the clothes you already have on? It would look pretty weird, just as a photograph of Beyoncé performing on stage with a caption about cake recipes beneath the picture would confuse readers. Everything you do needs to make sense in context.

There are other urban entertainment blogs out there, but Concrete Loop stands out because it has its own identity and personality. Concrete Loop *is* Angel Laws and Angel Laws *is* Concrete Loop, and my readers know that. You want your blog to also have a personal touch in order to stand out from the competition. There is only one "you" and your blog's topic and approach need to reflect that. You also need to make your topic immediately clear on every page. Readers going to your site should know as soon as the page opens what blog they're on (yours) because they'll be checking out all of the top blogs on subjects that interest them. You want yours to rise above the pack.

Earlier I told you to make a list of your top five interests in order to find a topic. But you can also use this list to scope out the competition. Do your homework and see what other blogs are covering those topics and how they're doing it. Competition is super important in this business. Simply because someone already writes about a subject doesn't mean you can't jump in too, but by looking at what others are doing, you might come up with a unique take on that subject that will set you apart from the rest. Plus, in order to stand out in crowded fields like entertainment or mommy blogging, you need to focus on originality and content.

After you check out what's already on the web in regards to similar content, you may decide to adjust or retool your approach. If your topic is already watered down or done to death, then maybe it's time to reconsider or at least to rethink it. Don't forget, if you narrow your focus down too much, it won't appeal to enough readers to make you any money. That means you need a good take on a strong topic that offers something for your core readers, but won't limit your readership to only a handful of people. Advertisers want broad appeal, but you can also go so broad that your blog loses focus.

Speaking of advertisers

Just as some subjects really attract the big bucks advertisers, others can have the opposite effect on your career and chase off advertisers. Anything that has to do with hate groups, prejudice, racism, or negativity is going to make advertising dollars disappear, not bring it in. And one advertising category—pornography—can make you money, but not in the sense you want to make money. I'd advise staying away from anything that might force traditional advertisers to scramble in the other direction.

This doesn't mean you can't be edgy and daring. You can. But you need to pick subjects that can be angled that way, not topics that make advertisers reconsider whether or not you fit their brands.

Also consider that your choice of subject will influence the types of advertising that you'll attract. If you blog about clothes and accessories, then hello shoe ads! If you cover sports, you're going to see sporting goods manufacturers beating a path to your blog. If you're talking travel, expect to earn rewards in the form of advertising revenue from hotels; foodies will get traffic from kitchen equipment manufacturers; and, mommy bloggers can expect ads from companies devoted to making products geared to kids, from clothes to over-the-counter pediatric medicines to toys. It's not rocket science, but it is something you need to factor into your game plan.

By angling your blog the right way, you can also pull in advertising dollars you might not necessarily expect. For example, if you blog about food but concentrate (angle it) on high-end fine dining, then your blog might appeal to vintners and the makers of premium crystal, linens, and china. You might also get the nod from expensive travel destinations, jewelry, and luxury cars. If you blog on sports, but angle it towards one particular consumer groups, say women, then you could attract manufacturers of workout gear, women's athletic shoes, and other products that are gender specific, like makeup, and bras. Angling your subject can mean multiplying your advertising reach.

But it can also mean losing some potential advertising. That fine-dining blog might have an ad for Rolex watches on it, but you're probably not going to see Taco Bell at the top the page. You need to carefully weigh all of your options, and then modify your approach the way it makes the most sense. For some, staying broad is the answer—it will open more advertisement avenues. But if you do, remember that the trade-off could be too much competition. You'll still have to find a way to make your blog stand out in the crowd.

The right mix

Your topic mix will continue to evolve and change with your blog, but you'll know when you've hit the right one because things will start coming together: Readers will pick up and advertisers will come calling. Blogging is not a static profession—like anything you do, what you blog about will shift as you explore the addition of new features and branch out into subjects that prove popular with your readers.

For Concrete Loop, I wanted to concentrate on black entertainers that weren't getting the press their talent should have brought to them: That was my "right mix" of subject and angle. One example of someone who wasn't getting much press was Drake, with his dope spin on rap and vocals. Originally from Canada, Drake wasn't as well-known here in the United States for his music when we started to cover him. Concrete Loop helped him out.

Of course Drake was already a star up north of our border for his role as Jimmy Brooks on the show *DeGrassi: The Next Generation*, but no other blogs were posting his mixtapes or talking about him when he started making music. We were one of the first to share his debut mixtape, and to cover and consistently do features on him. Now he's a big star, performing with Jay-Z and Kanye West, selling out tours, and performing on the VMAs.

One of the greatest joys I get from blogging is that I have discovered I have an eye for finding hot talented people who fly under the radar, like up-and-coming singer/songwriter Mateo—he's a performer with a lot of potential and Concrete Loop often features him. We create exposure for Mateo, and in the process, we also help his career—a win-win-win: one for us, one for him, and one for you Concrete Loop readers.

Artists we blog about print our posts along with the comments and use those to show record companies, which also helps them shop their music.

Singer/songwriter Mateo (L), producer Krucial (R), pictured with me in the recording studio.

I also know the companies come to Concrete Loop to see what our readers think of these artists—it makes me feel really good to know that we're not only bringing talented singers to our readers, but helping their careers as well.

Four blogs I think have it right

Personally, I think the number one example of the right way to do it is Concrete Loop. But there are a lot of great bloggers out there who have successfully made the leap from idea to blogging to making money because they found the right combination of subject and angle. Let me share with you my picks and why I like them.

1. JUSTJARED.COM

   Blogger Jared Eng started his blog a few months before I started Concrete Loop, and he focused more on mainstream celebs and music. I remember visiting his blog in the early days and it would crash or not load. Now he brings in millions of hits (no crashing), big advertisers, and exclusives with A-list stars.

2. DLISTED.COM

   Blogger Michael K. also started his blog in 2005. He is known for putting a humorous spin on the entertainment world. Most people prefer his blog over Perez Hilton when it comes to keeping it real about celebs. Even though he can be very blunt at times, he is still pulling in the big bucks with advertisers. He's a great example of finding a subject he liked and angling it.

3. FASHIONISTA.COM

   Founded by the creator of Gawker.com, Elizabeth Spiers, this blog focuses on fashion and trends, money-saving fashion tips, and more. Not only is it popular, but advertisers seem to love them.

4. MASHABLE.COM

   Also started in 2005, this web culture and news website is one of the best online. Creator Pete Cashmore generates millions of hits per day and was listed as *Forbes* magazine's top web celebs. The site is often known for breaking news stories from around the world and I think that's pretty good for someone who started the site from his home at the age of nineteen.

So now that you have your subject (hopefully) and example of great sites, let's move on to my second law, it's all in the name.

Angel's Second Law:
It's All in the Name

You've got it—an outstanding topic for your blog. You've researched, honed, refined, and angled it so it will stand out in the crowd. It reflects your passion and you know the subject will never bore you. Great. Now you need to find a name that will entice readers to take a look. How can you do that? Through a combination of exploration, imaginative thinking, and good old-fashioned trial and error—that's how.

Naming a blog can seem easy until you look at the thousands upon thousands of blogs out there. Some have clever insider names like Heather Armstrong's Dooce.com, which is a word Armstrong made up and then parlayed into a career after she was fired for blogging about her employers. As I said before, Concrete Loop is conceptual: I'm not a skateboarder or in construction. It represents what I want my blog to stand for—keeping readers in the "loop" with solid, bankable "concrete" information.

Others are more literal, like personal blogs that reflect the names of the blog owners or blogs that relate to specific professions, interests, or hobbies. But where it used to be easy to grab your own name or basic blog name, the sheer volume of blogs means that many of the best ones are now taken. In fact, finding a name that reflects who you are and what you do in the blogging world can be a huge challenge as more and more people jump in with blogs of their own.

But don't let that discourage you. Once you have the concept in mind, it's only a short path to the right name. And maybe you already have a good idea—or two—for a name that's unique and says it all. If so, then you still need to do your research and make sure the name you want isn't already taken. Many of the most creative ones are—and some basic blog names have been snapped up by companies and individuals who then turn around and try to sell those names (usually at really inflated prices) in order to make money. Here's a good tip: Even if you don't plan to use your own name as a domain name or blog, find out if it's available and buy it anyway. In fact, if you have a future project in mind and a good name for it, it's not such a bad idea (and very inexpensive too) to purchase that domain name against the time you'll use it. I did that with my personal blog, Angel on Fire (www.angelonfire.com). It's a small investment that can pay off big-time down the road

In any case, when purchasing a domain name, try for the .com as opposed to the other extensions (which don't get the same initial volume of traffic). Purchase it if it's available, and then park it until you're ready to develop it. Thinking ahead can mean the difference between snatching up a potentially useful web address and wishing you hadn't dragged your feet. Think about it; I purchased Concreteloop.com for $5 and now I'm making a living off of the site. You can also search around the web for coupon codes (www.GoDaddy.com is good for those) and that can help cut the price to next to nothing.

Why buy your name or another domain if you're not going to use it now? Because when you do make it big, you want that domain to be yours. Even if your plans change, you can always use it to redirect to your blog or other online businesses. Here's another tip: If what you want is currently not available, keep checking back because domains open up all of the time—people go out of business, lose interest, and, in some cases, simply forget to renew their domains. In fact, sometimes those domain names are even up for sale by their current owners for reasonable prices. So if you really are set on obtaining a particular domain, be prepared to move in and buy it the second it's available. And remember, if there's a domain you want, keep watching for it and be ready to pounce the minute it's available.

What not to name your blog

Before we talk more about naming your blog, let's look at the pitfalls of picking the wrong name and what you should avoid. First, steer clear of profane or negative words. The reason isn't prudish, but instead financial: They scare off advertisers. Typically, advertisers avoid spending their advertising budgets on sites with negative content and less-than-family-friendly names. That doesn't mean that you can't use inappropriate language or express your opinions on your blog, but you don't want to turn an advertiser off right from the beginning. So calling your blog something that automatically reinforces negativity or doesn't align with certain brands is only going to make potential advertisers click through to another blog, giving that blog the profit that could have been yours. Remember, *you may only have one chance to impress certain advertisers before they move on*, so first impressions can make all the difference.

Another aspect of naming your blog is to consider the length of the name and whether it is memorable or a pain to remember. This doesn't mean your blog can't have a unique or unusual name, but if no one can remember it, then you're not going to have a whole lot of repeat traffic. If you're blogging just for the fun of it or using your blog to share your life and thoughts with a special group of friends and not trying to monetize it, then you can afford to choose something oblique or esoteric with a peculiar spelling or that's challenging to recall. But if you want traffic outside of that close circle to beat a virtual path to your door, then you need to pick something that will resonate with them and, most important of all, will stick in their memories. A long convoluted string of letters won't get you there.

This means resisting the urge to call your blog some variation of www. angelwastestimeonstupidstuff.com or www.xyzandlotsofotherletters.com. Believe me, you'll stand a better chance of becoming a blog that people and advertisers find irresistible.

Human nature tips us towards things that roll off our tongues, or in this case embed themselves in our memories because they're catchy or have some other quality that makes them easy to remember—like a combination of words that is unique (Concrete Loop or Angelonfire fit that description), or a web address that can be quickly typed. Face it, it's a lot easier to type in www.yahoo.com or www.google.com and hit "send" than www.shereesultimatefashionistasheadquarters.com. Most people don't want to spend the time trying to remember long, complicated URLs and they won't bother if getting there is too much of a journey. Go for brief, easy to remember, and unique over long, hard to recall, and clunky.

But don't overthink it either

While it's important to have a good name, it's also important not to overthink the name. It's much more critical to get up and running and building traffic than to spend weeks trying to conjure up something that rings your bell. Overthinking can be like bread dough that you knead too much: If you keep fooling with it, it won't rise, and instead will be too chewy to enjoy, as well as indigestible. Same thing with a name that you've worked too hard to come up with; instead of something that flows and is easy to remember, if you try to be too clever, you'll only end up with a name that won't go the distance.

But do be original. Names based on blogs that are already established are not only bad form in the blogging world, but they also tend to make people mad. For example, some guy bought a variation of Concrete Loop and tried to sell it back to me. Not only did I not buy it, but also the last time I checked, he no longer owned it. I guess there were no takers for the faker.

That doesn't mean you can't use a concept that's already out there. You can take a broader idea and turn it into an original blog name by adding a word or two. For example, there are tons of ways to use the word *celebrities* in a blog's name simply by adding words like *online* or *the* or various combinations of words. If you're doing a mommy blog, you can convey your blog's message by the way you combine *kids, children, mom, mommy, mama,* or the many variations of those words. Like I said before, use your imagination, and remember, your name should reflect who you are, but not be so cryptic that it takes a codebook to figure it out.

What's in a name?

If you want to look at how important naming is to brand, turn to the entertainment world. Celebrities (or their teams) are geniuses at coming up with names that catch the eye, rule the imagination, and make you want to find out what they are about. Consider the Black Eyed Peas' will.i.am. He uses a clever kind of Dr. Seuss take on a common name to make it all his. Or Diddy, who has used variations of his name, but is readily identifiable with just that one word. Some people are simply blessed with great, catchy names—singer Janelle Monae's name is officially Janelle Monae Robinson—and others, following in Diddy's footsteps, such as Big Boi and Lady Gaga, adopt stage names.

Speaking of Janelle Monae, the dynamic young singer was always one of our favorites here at Concrete Loop. She's a very talented performer and was, in fact, the first celebrity interview we ever conducted for Concrete Loop. That was when her career was in its infancy. Now she's in commercials for major corporations like Target and Gap and is touring, as well as working on new music. You may have seen her performing her smash hit "Tightrope" for ABC's *Dancing with the Stars.*

I met Janelle and her band at a recent concert and she showed Concrete Loop the same love we've shown to her over the years. She even remembered that she was our first celeb interview! It made me proud that she gave Concrete Loop those exclusives. It's nice when celebs turn out to be good people who appreciate their fans and the people who gave them breaks along the way—and sad when celebrities don't remember the people who helped them out when they were up-and-coming.

Entertainer Janelle Monae
with Angel in September 2010
during fashion week.

PHOTO: Taj Washington

The overall package

While it's true that your blog's name alone won't make or break you, it is part of the total package when it comes to your success, and its importance in the overall picture can't be discounted, especially as you develop your brand. If you want your blog to be both a reader and advertiser magnet, then every detail is important, from the concept to the name to the layout. No one thing will guarantee success: It's all in the package. However, each component moves you forward or backward. It's up to you to decide what direction it will take.

Before we get to those points, there's another consideration to keep in mind when deciding on a name: SEO. SEO stands for search engine optimization and it's what helps drive traffic to your blog. The more traffic you have, the more you will attract, which leads to more buzz, and, most important of all, advertising dollars.

In a future chapter I will explain all about how SEO works and why you want to keep it in mind at all times—even when choosing a name. Also keep in mind that a name that incorporates SEO can help keep your blog popping up in searches. I won't analyze how SEO works here since you'll get the full lesson soon, but it's worth mentioning that SEO should play a part even when looking at a title or domain name. If there's some built-in high-traffic SEO in your title, it can keep your numbers bubbling upwards, and that's the right direction no matter what your goals.

Here are a few blogs I think are well named

Before we take on SEO, though, let's pause a few moments to look at blogs I think have clever, solid, insightful, and advertiser-friendly names, along with the reasons I like each one:

1. AFROBELLA.COM
   AfroBella is a blog dedicated to showing the beautiful side of natural hair and skin care. Creator Patrice Yursik reviews beauty products, attends seminars, and conducts interviews pertaining to the topic. I just think the name she chose is a great catchy spin on her subject matter.

2. WEBCREME.COM
   This blog is dedicated to posting links and images of blogs, sites, and designers that inspire both readers and the blog's owners. It's especially good if you're into web design and need a change of pace from the ordinary. Instead of using the word "content," they inserted creme and it has a nice ring to it.

3. CRUNKTASTICAL.NET

   Created by Fresh, this blog is has a humorous spin on urban entertainment. The title is catchy and most importantly, easy to remember.

4. WHOWHATWEAR.COM

   A bright and colorful fashion blog that makes clever use of spelling (who, what, where) and has lots and lots of photographs. Nice way to bend a word and come up with a clever title.

   And, while we're talking about names, you will want to consider the issue of branding while naming your blog. You'll see how branding can impact your blog's success (and how the name relates to your branding efforts) in a chapter later on in the book.

Angel's Third Law:
Get Down to Work

Blogging about celebrities brings me tons of collateral benefits. And because I make it a point to cover all aspects of celebrities' lives—from their music to their parties, tours, and personal lives—I am often invited to special events. I keep Concrete Loop updated and relevant by adding new features that, in turn, increase both my personal expertise and my experience. When I brought celebrity fashion to Concrete Loop's lineup, it afforded me a chance to meet famous designers and receive invitations to cover dream fashion events like New York City's Mercedes-Benz Fashion Week. I'm not going to lie though—Fashion Week is very draining, and honestly, after a while all those collections tend to blur together. By the end, I've found that once you've seen one fashion show, you've pretty much seen them all.

Still, it's fun to see the rich and famous lining the front rows at different shows, and naturally, since they're attending the city's premiere fashion events, they're dressed to kill. That alone provides reams of material for Concrete Loop's readers. And since I attend these shows in person, I've learned a lot about the world of high fashion. I also know that the overall theme of these collections is not always so obvious and you have to pay close attention to really "get" some couture collections. Couture collection themes can be very clever and restrained, and in some cases even hidden.

At one show I attended, I noticed that the designer had built her collection around flowers: The colors, the shapes, and silhouettes of the garments on the runway, as well as the presentation itself, all brought in a floral theme that wouldn't be obvious to the casual observer. You had to really pay attention to recognize how cohesive that designer's collection was. That's a subtlety that

Designer Nicole Miller, model Cassie, and Angel during a Fashion Night Out event in New York City.

PHOTO: Taj Washington

designers can get away with, but upcoming bloggers can't emulate, particularly when it comes to SEO. It pays to be bold when developing SEO.

That's one of the main points we're going to touch on in this chapter, along with another important decision you have to make—the choice of platform. Since we mentioned SEO in the last chapter when we dipped into naming your blog, we'll start there. (If you need help with any of the technical terms I use in this chapter, flip to the short glossary at the end of the book.)

Raising your visibility

Keeping SEO in mind as you build your blog can help you get off to a faster start trafficwise. And face it—traffic is the name of the game, particularly when it comes to attracting advertisers. A lot of companies offer SEO and website promotion, but you don't need to hire someone as you can do this on your own, so my advice is not to waste your money. Learn how to research and recognize SEO words and the right placement for them. It's a valuable skill.

By the way, SEO is considered "organic." That's because it helps increase your rankings in search results without costing you anything (but time). The benefits of doing your homework when it comes to SEO are obvious: If people can find you via search engines, they will visit your blog and your page views will go up. Once again, the higher statistics will draw companies and their advertising dollars to your site. Turning a blog into a moneymaker starts with visibility.

How do you find the right words to make your blog pop up at the top of searches (especially Google searches)? Start with making a list of SEO words that pertain to your site and then know where—and how—to place those words on your blog.

How to find the words you need to know

Consider your potential readership: Remember that how they approach a search is everything in the world of SEO. Take, for example, an imaginary food blog with lots of recipes. Perhaps you might call a recipe for a rice casserole, "Felicia's Mom's Fabulous Veggie Rice." How many of your visitors are going to type that phrase into a search engine? Probably none.

That means you need to think like someone who is looking for a fabulous veggie rice dish. That probably would translate out to words like *rice*, *casserole*, *vegetarian*, and perhaps some of the ingredients you use, but not *Felicia's Mom*.

How do you come up with keywords that *will* work for you? Start by using research tools that will help you find proven keywords for blog subjects. One of the best of these is the Google AdWords Keyword Tool.

The Google AdWords Keyword Tool searches keywords for you and provides data on how well these words, and variations on them, do in searches. For example, entering the term *celebrities* brings up literally millions of search hits; that list is then refined down to search categories like *latest celebrity gossip, black celebrity gossip, celebrity photos,* and on and on through various search permutations. From this you can tell which versions of the word *celebrities* are most popular in searches.

Remember that popular terms are going to rise and fall with the news, too: When Kanye West interrupted Taylor Swift at the VMAs and stated that Beyoncé deserved Swift's award, all three performers—and the VMAs—shot up in the search rankings. Remember—what's at the top of the news rotation is also going to be what's at the top of Internet searches. It's also good to keep that in mind as you continue to add content to your blog. By bringing in a touch of whatever is hot at the moment, you can raise your numbers.

When looking at keywords, you also want to remember to convey who you are and what you offer. You can put Beyoncé's name on all of your pages and you will get some hits—at first. But unless you host a Beyoncé-only fan blog, you need to incorporate other keywords that will transmit what your blog is all about. And don't be too broad or too narrow; either approach can get your blog lost in the forest of keyword searches.

Celebrities and their publicists are pretty savvy at keeping their names in front of the press, but even they understand that saturation can make people grow weary of you. Take a look at what happened when Ben Affleck was dating Jennifer Lopez (remember "Bennifer"?): They were in the news so much that even their fans were tired of them. Like overexposed celebs, you can repeat SEO-grabbing content to the extent that you turn your blog into a repetitive snoozefest for your readers. Be careful not to overdo a good thing.

Other places to put keywords

Keywords don't simply belong in the content. You should also use keywords to aid site navigation, describe the page, as text stand-in for images, and in your meta and anchor tags. Let's briefly touch on all of these concepts as they relate to SEO:

1. Site Navigation: Your site navigation is not only crucial to search engine results placement, but it also conveys your priorities and interests. It's important for you to set up intuitive navigation that is both logical and easy to understand.

2. Page Description: Organize your content so it's clean and your keywords are current and accurate.
3. Text Stand-In for Images: You should always use a text stand-in for images since they not only identify what should be there if the image doesn't load, but can also act as keywords.
4. Meta and Anchor Tags: Create additional keyword opportunities with links and better search engine opportunities.

Grab those opportunities!

Earlier I mentioned that staying on top of newsworthy opportunities increases your visibility and jacks up your page hits. You should also look at the SEO opportunities you can translate from your everyday life.

Let's say you are out for dinner and in walks Beyoncé and Jay-Z. No matter what kind of blog you have, mentioning where you saw them, what they ate, what she was wearing, and other little details can boost your page views on many levels. That can lead to new readers and a better shot at advertising dollars because millions of people each day search for news and gossip about Beyoncé, Jay-Z, and other celebrities who are top news-makers.

Another good place to see what's hot and provide opportunities for you to add to your visibility and SEO worthiness is Google's blog search (www.blogsearch.google.com), which gives you instant access to the hottest blog topics at the moment. By looking at what is charting well on Google, you can jump on the bandwagon and write your own original posts about things and people of current interest to your potential audience. You can also link from those posts to your own blog, which will drive traffic your way.

Google Analytics

This is a good place to introduce you to Google Analytics, which is a cost-free Google tool. Like many of Google's services, it's user-friendly and a great way to measure your traffic and get to know exactly who is visiting your blog and why. It also gives you an accurate snapshot of how long your visitors are spending on your site and where. That allows you to zero in on your blog's most popular features and replicate them in the future in order to keep those visitors coming back.

What Google Analytics does is generate traffic stats about your blog. It lets you know where your visitors originate (from search engines, links, or other portals) and can work with AdWords (which I cover in detail in Angel's Sixth Law) to help track advertising particulars.

As for SEO in general, a lot of people think that with the new, more intuitive Google search, SEO is not important anymore. I don't agree. While I don't think SEO is as crucial as it was two years ago, it's still a game changer and one that any blogger who wants to make money via blogging should factor into both the design and follow-through.

On to your platform

Celebrities generally rely on their stylists to look both attractive and memorable. Rihanna is noted for her quirky fashion sense, but really the one calling the shots is her stylist. I always thought Rhianna was a real trendsetter, but like most celebs, she only looks as good as her stylist is talented. That shouldn't be too surprising since that's a stylist's job: to make the celebrity stand out: and BE hot or trendy or sometimes even terrible. Yes, I said "terrible." Looking like a hot mess isn't always a bad thing because it can get you onto all of the big entertainment blogs, as well as on TV (and who wouldn't want to be ripped apart in front of millions by Joan Rivers and the Fashion Police team?). In the dog-eat-dog world of attracting press coverage, even negative coverage can be a positive. In my opinion, when her stylist dresses her, Rihanna looks entirely different than when she dresses herself. Like I said, a good stylist is really the trendsetter here, not the star.

Just as the stylist works with the raw material he or she has (the celebrity), bloggers also have to turn raw material into something memorable, searchable, and solid. One of the most important considerations when embarking on a blogging career is absolutely critical to the blogger's success: You must pick a good platform. To me the decision was ultra simple: WordPress is my hands-down favorite.

But before I go into detail about why I like WordPress so much, let me say a word or two about setting your blog up on one of the big blogging sites like Tumblr or Blogspot. There are pros and cons associated with both, but in my opinion, the cons outweigh the pros.

Here's the issue for me: First, Google doesn't target their searches to the big blog hosts. If I search for Beyoncé and you have something about her on your blog, of course it will show up on a blog search. However, if your blog is hosted on a dot-com domain, you'll have the advantage of surfacing on regular keyword searches. Picking up search engine hits on a blog hosted on LiveJournal, Blogspot, Blogger, or others is more difficult than if your blog is hosted on your own domain. (Google and other search engines do have blog-only searches, though, so you are still searchable, just not as likely to pick up traffic from regular, nonblog specific Google searches.)

Screencap of my personal blog, www.angelonfire.com, which is hosted by Tumblr.

Another argument in favor of having your blog on a dot-com as opposed to a popular blog platform site is that blogs on places like Tumblr, Blogspot, and the others have limited bandwidth options. Anyone who has a Tumblr blog knows they are notorious for always having bandwidth and server problems, causing many blogs to be down for hours or days. That means your blog is losing visibility and potential readers during that downtime. Now imagine if your blog takes off. It's sort of an oblique punishment for being successful. Don't get me wrong, I actually use Tumblr as a hosting agent for my personal blog, www.angelonfire.com, but it's frustrating when you try to edit or create a post and the site is down. And if you are trying to create a blog that generates revenue, that is a big deal.

Another drawback to having your blog hosted on one of the popular blogging sites is that eventually you will want to change over to a domain (take my word for it—if you are blogging to make money, this is inevitable). Moving all of your posts and content is both tedious and time-consuming. You're much better off doing it the right way from the beginning.

And one additional benefit to starting with your own domain is that you won't experience redirecting from the host site (i.e., www.angelonfire.tumblr.com). It looks more professional when you just have the .com behind your name, especially to advertisers. (See a theme here?) Starting on a domain helps you initiate the branding process right from the outset. We'll talk about branding in detail in a future chapter, but it's something you should always keep in the back of your mind. For a blogger, especially one who wants to make some serious money, branding should always be a factor.

I would also like to note that early on I was nearly put out of business before I even really got into business because of exceptionally high traffic. While it was gratifying to score all of those page views, having to come up with so much money all at once was tough, as well as unexpected. All this happened while I was under a domain, but in the long run it was a great learning lesson about knowing your bandwidth limits. You will avoid this issue if you know your bandwidth allowances ahead of time and discuss each package with your host.

Now, back to WordPress—let's compare it to Blogspot and other free blogging programs out there.

WordPress versus the rest

To me, the best thing about WordPress (www.wordpress.org) is that it's simple to use. It has a program you can download right onto your server, it adapts to a dot-com or domain with minimal problems, and it's easy to customize.

WordPress also has themes—you click one button for the layout and upload it, thus avoiding all of the coding you have to do with Blogspot, Tumblr, and others. The comments, posting, and layout are all really easy to use on the backend, especially when you're first starting out. Tumblr and Blogspot are also organized on the backend, but in my opinion their free layouts do not work well in terms of commercial blogging; most look like the kind of commercial layouts you usually get from free hosting. With Word-Press you get the best of both worlds: a professional looking layout that is also free.

These days bloggers have a lot of choices, so make certain you do your homework before you commit to a platform. For example, a lot of bloggers complain that Tumblr goes down when the traffic is heavy, and if you're trying to post, you can lose the whole thing. This could be an issue if you can't get new content up in a timely manner. Another thing to consider is the backend. Personally, I found that Blogspot's backend wasn't as sophisticated or easy to use as I wanted it to be, although that may have changed in the past few years.

A word here about Tumblr, which incorporates a one, two, three approach. You sign up and you have an account. You don't have to worry about uploading to the FTP or uploading all of the coding like WordPress does. All of the free blog hosting sites are pretty easy on the backend, but I think it's smarter to simply go with WordPress from the beginning because once you start attracting a readership, you will also start getting more comments. It's really annoying when your site blows up and you're on another platform, and you want to transfer all of those posts and comments. I know because I went through this more than one time. In the long run you don't want to transfer all these files. It's counterproductive and cuts into down your personal time.

If it sounds like I am a WordPress groupie, I guess I am. I recommend it because it has always worked for my blog. Let's summarize the features that I think sets WordPress apart from the pack:

- Easy to transfer and upload files
- Plug-ins have dozens of features
- A vast collection of stylized themes to choose from
- Frequent upgrades to fix any bugs
- Good community support where you can post any questions you might have
- Better vehicle for branding—your work looks more professional
- Additional plug-ins for advertisers where you don't have to do the coding (like Google Adsense)
- Can master features through trial and error

I want to talk a little bit more about that last one. Blogging is all about learning what works best for you and your blog. When I first started, I had a feature that would link comments to past posts and readers told me it was repetitive, so I stopped doing that. WordPress is very fluid and adaptable. It lets you change your approach as you learn what works for your readership, and what doesn't.

As you continue to blog, you will learn how to write and edit code, and each time you post with WordPress, you will also be gaining in knowledge along the way. For example, when I first started blogging, one of the big stories I covered was when best-selling author Terry McMillan (author of *Waiting to Exhale* and many more books) was on *The Oprah Winfrey Show* and she was talking about how she found out her husband was gay. That generated a lot of comments, some of which were derogatory and hurtful. With WordPress I could moderate unacceptable comments with ease, which comes in handy when you've got a post you know is going to generate a lot of attention or controversy.

Those comments not only make Concrete Loop a more interesting place to be, but they also help me understand my audience. And that's what the next chapter is all about.

Angel's Fourth Law:
Know Who Loves Ya

A lot of people may not know this but Diddy has always supported Concrete Loop and often spends a lot of money bringing high-profile advertising campaigns our way. So you will probably be surprised to know that we have had many disagreements over his coverage and feedback on the site. Back in 2009, he had purchased a lot of ads promoting a new video and one of them was a blog wrap—which is a regular post with an advertisement wrapped around it. We published the video as we normally do and of course some people didn't like it. They basically clowned him and ripped the video to shreds in the comment area.

Later that evening, one of Diddy's many assistants called me with a list of negative comments he wanted removed from the site and I told her that I don't remove comments in that way. If someone is stating his or her opinion in a legitimate way, then the comment stays whether it is negative or positive. His employee then got an attitude and pretty much hung up the phone on me.

A few moments later she called back and asked if I would talk to Diddy and I said, sure, why not? Diddy said he didn't want to come at me disrespectfully, but he didn't realize what he paid for was to get clowned and roasted on the website. I told him he didn't pay to be clowned, he paid for a blog wrap post and that's what he got. I had to explain to him what the separation between editorial and advertising was and he said he respected my stance, was new to the online world, and was just trying, in his words, "to crack the code."

Before we hung up the phone, we pretty much came to an understanding about the whole thing. I thought it was pretty dope that he understood it was my website and no one can buy me, and as a matter fact he is still a big supporter of Concrete Loop. Real recognizes real.

So how does this all tie into the name of this chapter? Well, Diddy's audience is also my audience, and just like it's important for an artist to know for whom he is playing, it's important for bloggers to understand their power, and, of course, respect their readership. If you don't know who your consumer is, then you won't produce a targeted product that will sell. As a blogger, it's up to you to figure out who you are writing for and dish up material that will keep them coming back.

How do you figure out your audience's identity? Let me tell you how I did it. My experience might save you a little time and trouble.

Learn as you go

There's no magic formula for figuring out your blog's demographics. It takes time for a steady readership to evolve, and sometimes you have to keep tweaking your material in order to make it appeal to certain types of readers. That means developing a blog can involve a lot of trial and error. It's like riding a bike: You start with a tricycle, move up to a little bike with training wheels, take off the training wheels and fall a little, then graduate to a big kid's bike, hand brakes and all. It's a gradual process that you have to learn to negotiate on your own.

Remember though that *you* are in control of your blog. The Concrete Loop audience is primarily eighteen- to thirty-four-year-old college-educated African American women, but that doesn't mean men don't read my blog—they do—and so do individuals of other races and age ranges. But my core readership is well-defined in my demographics.

This is important for two reasons: Your demographics help you choose content and also attract advertisers. And, most important of all, your blog is a reflection of who you are. Your core readership should be individuals with whom you can empathize and relate.

A matter of control

While it's important to stay current and keep SEO in mind as you blog, it's even more important to stay true to yourself. That means blogging about subjects you understand and relate to because to do otherwise will ring false to your readers. Never underestimate the intelligence and depth of the people who read your blog. Also remember—they are patronizing your blog because it covers a subject about which they are interested; and if they are interested, then they keep up with the subject matter. If you don't know much about it, not only will your ignorance show, but also you'll lose the very readers you're hoping to turn into your core audience.

Knowing your audience isn't simply a matter of recognizing who your readership is, but it's also about knowing what your readership likes and dislikes. For example, Concrete Loop is known for being a generally positive blog, so if I started posting about Beyoncé in a dirty, scandalous way, people would ask me why I was being so negative toward her. If I went after celebrities like some other bloggers do, I think the majority of my readers would pack up and go home.

There are celebrity blogs that capitalize on the mean and cruel side of this business, but Concrete Loop does not share that approach. My readers want to keep up with their favorites and pick up a little insider's glimpse of their lives, but they don't want to read trash talk about them. That doesn't mean I can't get a little spicy once in a while. I'm not out to be all sweetness and light here, but in the same vein, I'm also not out to slam everyone and take cheap shots. Please believe me when I say I have stories for days and do share some of them, but I believe that if you knowingly put negative energy out there, it will come back to you two- or threefold.

Lover not a fighter

No one likes to find out that what they may regard as a good relationship is really something else. As a blogger I often meet performers I admire. What a disappointment it is to find out that some have attitude problems! That is one of the downsides of my part of the business. It messes up your whole perception of them both as artists and as individuals. One performer that comes to mind is neosoul artist Musiq SoulChild. Growing up, I was a big admirer of him and his music, and when I learned I landed an exclusive phone interview with him, I was ecstatic. But from the beginning of the interview something was off with him; every question I asked would evoke a condescending response. Even when I asked questions coming directly from his fans on the blog, he still had a smug vibe. While I was doing the interview, I thought, 'Hey, what *is* your problem?' I was a big fan, but after that interview, I was really turned off, and I never listened to his music the same way.

Another example is R&B singer Trey Songz. We also had a phone interview that got kind of heated less than thirty seconds in. He came at me and said I was the blogger who talked negatively about him. I told him, "No, Concrete Loop is a positive blog, we actually support you." He said, no, that he could have sworn it was my blog, and then he said, "Let's get on with the interview."

I stopped him and asked him for an example of where I said something negative about him, and he said again to just get on with the interview. I said, "You can't give me an example because you know there's not one. You're mixing me up with another blog or you're confusing the comments section with the blog." Then he got really quiet and asked me, "Are we going to do the interview, or are we going to do the interview?"

I know I should step outside of the box and say to myself, it's just a business. They were both probably having an off day. I shouldn't take things so personally. But you can't help but be disillusioned when you respect or look up to someone and they don't respect you, your time, or your business. The fact that some celebrities cop an attitude when Concrete Loop has always supported them and their careers in a positive light is something that continually irks me.

It was very obvious that Trey Songz and Musiq Soulchild didn't understand Concrete Loop or our readers. I could have put both of them on blast and generated a bunch of hits, but I decided to take the positive approach and focus on their upcoming projects instead of how they treated me behind the scenes. Blogging is all about the readers trusting you to stay true to yourself and your blog's philosophy. What it's *not* about is phoniness and trying to be something you're not. Readers know the difference and expect consistency and understanding. If Musiq Soulchild or Trey Songz had done their research, they'd know what my blog and its readers are all about. Concrete Loop supports artists—point-blank, period, end of discussion.

Posting for dollars

Sure, you want to make money from your blog. That's why you're reading this book. But you also want to be sure your heart is in your posts and that you're not blogging only as a way to make money. A blog that's only about cash won't stay alive for long. Readers know passion when they see it—and also recognize when it's missing.

Two big mistakes I often see are bloggers who post as space fillers on slow days, and posts that are only there to cater to the advertiser. Both can be the kiss of death for a blog because neither reflects your audience's needs.

Posting just to fill up the page waters down your content and your readership. Who wants to go to a blog that's full of space holders? It's kind of like what your mama used to tell you about bad-mouthing people: If you don't have anything good to say, then keep your mouth shut. Only the blog version of that is, if you don't have anything to write about, then don't write it.

If you're occupying Internet real estate just to do it, then readers will get that and they won't come back for more. Make your posts meaningful and relevant to them. Otherwise, you're messing with their time as well as your own. Looking at it from a fashion perspective, it's like owning a whole dresser full of $5 scarves or one to-die-for designer scarf. What choice would you make? Most would choose quality over quantity, and you should make sure you keep that in mind.

The same goes for selling yourself for advertising dollars. Like I told Diddy, I'm not for sale. You shouldn't be either. If you change your blogging style in order to accommodate advertisers, you'll lose your identity.

I'm not saying you shouldn't blog to attract advertisers, but there are ways to be true to yourself and also work with advertisers. You must separate editorial from advertising. To endorse a product or write a glowing review of something because you've been paid to do so is not only dishonest, but also insulting to your readers.

Money is good, but it shouldn't be your sole inspiration for posts.

Relating to your readers

Many of my readers have been with me since the beginning and they've grown with Concrete Loop. Better than anyone, these longtime readers know who I am and understand my brand. Your readers will also learn what and who you are through your blogging. Think of your audience in the sense of growing with them instead of being another hit on your Google Analytics chart.

When I was invited to represent Concrete Loop at the African American Online Summit at the White House (read more about this in the next chapter), I posted about it and got tons of comments from my longtime readers about how much the blog has grown. They care about Concrete Loop and I care about what they think. It's a form of mutual respect.

This isn't to say that your blog and interests can't change over time. Mine did. I started Concrete Loop as a fun, hobby sort of thing and even included some personal stuff on there, but as the blog evolved, I started listening to what my readers said and watching to see which posts drew the most comments. Hands down, it was the celebrity coverage that turned out to be the most popular.

I also know my demographics and that my readers don't want to come to the blog to hear me preach about sexuality or religion. It turns them off. We do cover politics, although that can be the kiss of death for your blog if you're not careful, unless you write a political blog. When I post about something political, I make sure to keep my personal opinions out of it and don't do too much backend commenting. The readers can take it to a personal level if they want in the comments—that's their choice. That's what makes them happy, and if they're happy, then so am I.

At the end of the day

Remember it's *your* blog, and that blog is your baby. Your readers need you and you need them. Concrete Loop became popular very fast. I have fans in Singapore, Tokyo, and Norway, and they aren't what you would call my prime demographic. However, they are still an important part of the site. You just never know who is reading your blog.

Angel's Fifth Law:
Be Original and Don't Bite

Imentioned in the previous chapter how, in the fall of 2010, I received an invitation (along with Concrete Loop contributor Jeffery "J. Dakar" Holley) to a bloggers' symposium at the White House. I thought it was a joke at first. I mean, my dad was in the Marine Corps for nearly three decades and he was never invited to the White House, so why would a blogger like me snag an invitation? I figured that either someone was clowning me or trying to scam me. I reported it as spam and thought nothing of it.

Me, pictured in front of the White House along with my name tag and official White House folder.

You can imagine my surprise later that week I was contacted again and discovered the invitation was indeed genuine. I've been a child entrepreneur, a grocery bagger, a cashier, a college student, and a bored skate park employee before going into full-time blogging and, face it, I started that as a hobby. I never expected it to grow into a livelihood, much less lead to meeting the president of the United States in his home on Pennsylvania Avenue.

Naturally, I was a little nervous. All of the big minority publications were represented, like *Essence* magazine. I felt humbled and honored to be included with such publications that have been in the game far longer than I.

Even more humbling was sitting in that round table and seeing President Barack Obama walk into the room. He was exactly what you would expect the most powerful man in the world to be: dignified, intelligent, warm, but gracious and very appreciative that we were there. I am so glad that I didn't miss the opportunity to take part in the symposium and meet him. It was the memory of a lifetime.

He went around the roundtable one by one shaking hands and talking to all the honored guests. In the process, I also got a chance to speak with him for a few moments, and he was very laid-back and comfortable in his own skin. Well versed in politics, he was very aware of both himself and his audience.

One thing that stood out about the summit was how well organized they were. Naturally, you expect the White House to be on top of things like this, and they don't disappoint. Every i was dotted and every t crossed. In addition to all of the security and background checks they must do, his staff leaves nothing to chance.

It's not a bad idea to take your cue from the White House if you want to succeed as a blogger. While the Obamas have a huge staff to make sure everything they do is perfect, you won't start out with a lot of help—at least at first. You have to do all of those things yourself. How do you keep your blog original, yet operate efficiently? Follow my three guiding principles and you'll produce a blog that's not only original, but also will reflect its author's good blogging habits. Let's take a look at those three principles and how you can put them to work for you.

Three principles you need to know

While it's good to ignore the rules in some instances (I did when I first started blogging—minority bloggers as a whole were both scarce and not terribly successful when I first hatched the idea for Concrete Loop), at some point you have to put some parameters in place or run the risk of being unfocused and fragmented, both in your approach to blogging and in your product. You can be innovative *and* creative, yet still incorporate quality standards. Think about how celebrities like Oprah Winfrey do this.

Oprah isn't simply one of the most talented individuals in the entertainment world, she is also a brilliant strategist. She and her team understand how to move the brand into new arenas and her entrepreneurial reach spans several industries, from magazines to movies, and now a network. And that doesn't even take into account her career as an actress, producer, production head, etc. How does she do it all and do it so well? In a business where flashes in the pan are as common as knockoff designer purse sellers on the streets of New York City, she obviously has both a great understanding of her brand (a subject which we will discuss in detail in Angel's Seventh Law), as well as how to keep lots of balls in the air without dropping any of them. Here's a hint on how she does it: not by chance.

Entrepreneurial giants like Oprah don't get where they are by being random. If you've ever seen a major A-list celebrity in action, you'll know that they work hard at getting where they are and double that effort to stay there. You need to do the same. Of course, when celebrities start making it big, they surround themselves with an efficient team, something you may not be able to afford or even need at the beginning. Instead, *you* are going to be your own team. Unlike Oprah or her best friend Gayle King, who both move in a wave of people, you're going to have to do it all. The bad news is that it is going to require discipline. The good news is that you *can* do it if you put your mind to it and follow my advice.

For me, there are three vital components that I made central to building my blog, and after all of these years I don't ever forget them when putting together Concrete Loop's posts and features. All three not only keep Concrete Loop fresh, but also keep my readers, as well as advertisers, coming back for more. They are as follows:

1. Organization
2. Consistency
3. Motivation

Let's take each component and dissect it, then look at what they can do for your blog.

Organization

Organization is probably one of the most overused words of this century. Almost every magazine aimed at women has an organization story on the cover (come to think of it, you never see organization stories for men—why is that?). Just hit the checkout at your favorite grocery store and there they are: 10 Ways to Get Organized Today, Organize Your Bathroom, How to Stay

Organized, and on and on. But being organized when it comes to your blog really isn't about putting macaroni in plastic storage containers, better ways to store your eye shadows and lipsticks, or making sure your shoes all point in the same direction. Instead, it's more about keeping your blog in order so readers can navigate it without losing their minds, interest, or curiosity.

You need to organize your content according to how you're going to post and present it, as well as when you post it. And it's imperative that you think ahead. While you are working on one post, consider how it fits in with the other material already on your blog, as well as what you already have in the pipeline as far as future posts and features are concerned. Try asking yourself these questions:

Four Questions You Should Ask about Every Post or Feature
1. How will all of this material integrate into my blog?
2. Is the material cohesive and does it fit the overall theme of my blog, or does the post give the impression it's been forced?
3. Do these posts reflect the direction in which I want to go?
4. Am I mapping out my direction or simply letting my blog wander all over the place?

While you're working on posts behind the scenes, you should also have content that's live, regardless of whether you're talking about celebrities, fashion, or food. This should be a never-ending cycle because having new stuff will not only attract readers, but also keep them clicking back to see what's been added. And readers can develop very high expectations, particularly if you set the bar high at the beginning—and it goes without saying that you should set that bar high.

Consistency

A couple of decades ago, Coca-Cola changed the formula and taste of its main product. It bombed big-time and drove consumers to demand the return of the old formula. Coke replied by reissuing original Coke as "Coke Classic." Some think it was a publicity ploy; others believe it was a huge miscalculation of Coke's target market. But whether the move was planned or not, it ultimately compromised Coke's brand.

One look at how consistency affects your shopping habits and you'll understand why it's so important to keep the quality of your work level. If you patronize a certain restaurant and you love their cheesecake, how would you feel if, after bragging about how good it tasted, you took a friend there and it tasted like it came straight from a box? Would you go back?

Would you stick with your favorite shoe manufacturer if it started pumping out shoes that fell apart a month after you bought them? I wouldn't and I'm betting you wouldn't either. Consistency isn't always about quality though. Variety is also a big player. How much would you patronize a store that rarely added new merchandise? Would you buy your clothes from a shop that carried nothing contemporary and remained mired in one decade? Nope, and if you let your site and content stay static and never put anything new up, you're going to disappoint and bore your readers. Trust me, I've been there.

I know we're talking about two different concepts here, but both embrace consistency. Let's separate and examine them more closely, starting with consistent quality.

Like the crappy piece of cheesecake or shoes that fell apart, a departure from your quality standards can lead to a drop-off in numbers. Toni Morrison writes about the lives of African American women and her readers expect a certain level of quality when they open her books. If the book is poorly written or doesn't live up to their expectations, they might not buy her next one. The same holds true with best-selling authors like Stephen King, Stephanie Meyer, and J. K. Rowling. They succeed because their readers expect certain things from them, and they consistently deliver.

That's exactly what happens with performers. Sure, even the best can have off nights. They're human. But audiences expect a high degree of quality when they're paying upwards of $100 to see their fave. Jay-Z would not sell out his concerts if his showmanship was unpredictable on stage, no matter how die-hard his fans may be. Staying consistent is what separates the ones who become household names and the ones who fade into has-been land.

You can't build a following without developing and adhering to certain standards, and without a following, you won't appeal to advertisers. Blogging for money is mostly about numbers. But keeping your quality consistent shouldn't be your only brush with that concept. You also need to post new stuff on a regular basis.

Getting back to the performer analogy, you might enjoy seeing an artist perform popular songs from early in their career, but you also want to hear new and current ones. Unless, of course, that particular entertainer is no longer producing new material and is on an oldie-but-goodie kind of tour. Not many readers are going to keep trekking to your blog to see the same old same old posted on it.

I can tell you from experience that not only does new material keep an audience loyal, but it can be habit-forming, in a good (for you) way. That's pretty much how Concrete Loop developed the loyal following it has today. I kept adding new things three or four times each day and readers returned to check it out three, four, even more times a day. A win for everyone.

Motivation

This one is hard because even though you may love your subject, sometimes staying motivated can be a real challenge, especially if you haven't started seeing decent returns on your investment; believe me, remaining motivated is the number one key to success if you want to turn your blog into a moneymaker.

Muhammad Ali, probably the greatest boxer the world has ever known, once said, "It's lack of faith that makes people afraid of meeting challenges, and I believed in myself." The three-time heavyweight champion of the world won a gold medal at the 1960 Summer Olympics, changed his name and religion, then stood in front of the world and refused to be inducted into the military and sent to Vietnam. Whether you think his stand was right or wrong, the point is he took it and refused to back down, even though he wasn't allowed to fight in the ring again for four years. If you look at his life and what he accomplished, you see a winner, not a quitter.

Many performers also started small and worked their ways up to stardom by remaining motivated and ambitious. In the case of a creative artist (which also describes bloggers), sometimes it's very hard to remain that way and keep on doing your best when it seems like no one "gets" you or what you're doing. I imagine even great creative minds like Picasso, Dickens, and Basquiat felt discouraged at times and found themselves without motivation. If it's sometimes hard to retain your drive, then you are in excellent company.

Never lose sight of why you started blogging in the first place. Keep your goals foremost in your mind. Did you start blogging as a hobby and hope to pick up some pocket change or are you serious about making money? Remember what prompted you to start your blog. Even though your overall goals may shift and change with time, don't lose sight of what first put your feet on this path. Adjust your goals as you change your focus, but don't let setbacks, time, or complacency push you away from your ultimate objectives.

In the early days of Concrete Loop, it was easy to lose sight of my own goals and sometimes hard to stay motivated, especially after I quit college and the money started to slow down. But I hung on and eventually my persistence paid off. You, too, can triumph over the slow times and reap the rewards.

Blogging can pay off in many ways. For me the payoff is both in money and side benefits. For instance, I get invited to a lot of music events, like studio sessions with up-and-coming artists—R&B singers, rappers, you name it. I was in the studio with Kanye West a couple of years ago when he was working on his fourth studio album, *808s & Heartbreak*. I saw the final mixing and had the opportunity to see how he works behind the scenes. I also met his team and spent a good four or five hours just chilling, eating cereal and fruit, watching everyone crack jokes, and play Super Nintendo while listening to the beats.

When I start feeling unmotivated, I remember being in that California studio, watching Kanye work, and realize exactly how far I've come—and how far I am going to go. I keep my eye on the prize and you should too. As good things come your way, press them into your mental scrapbook and pull them out when you're feeling unmotivated. Like my studio visits do for me, your high moments can bring you validation and remind you that hard work pays in many ways.

Another thing to remember is that staying motivated can be more diffi-cult over the long run. When you first start blogging, you're usually enthu-siastic and ready to conquer the world. As time passes, your motivation will probably lag a bit. Hang in there. Blogging isn't a short-term, once-and-done

Kanye West and producer No I.D. in the studio, October 2008.

PHOTOGRAPH BY: Angel Laws

kind of thing. It takes commitment to keep going, and even the best bloggers sometimes find their motivation flagging.

Prior to making the decision to commercialize your blog, recognize that in order to succeed, you are going to have to work harder than you've ever worked before in order to make it. You have to go 100 percent, 24/7, and if that bothers you, then you may not be cut out for professional blogging. I'm not going to lie—it's a hard job, but also a fun one most of the time. That said, you are going to have to get used to not having much of a personal life, at least in the beginning.

I was talking to a friend the other day about the lack of personal time in my own life. As I'm writing this, my DVR is almost at 100 percent capacity, and I haven't had the chance to watch my shows in ages. But to me that's a small price to pay for success, and if I had to do it all over again, I would still blog.

The motivation can be found inside you. You just have to want it enough.

Nude pictures as a business decision? You bet!

If you're not planning on making money from your blogging, then you don't need to worry about basing decisions on how advertisers will react. But if you're hoping to monetize your blog, even if it's just earning some pocket change, then you need to treat every decision as a business decision. That's what the stars do, even when it appears they've had an "oops" moment.

Kanye West and Rihanna are smart and so are their teams. They know that if you want to promote a project, you have to be everywhere, so they always come up with publicity stunts or some type of attention-grabbing ploy. Think about all of the nude or scantily dressed pictures, sex tapes, and videos of celebrities cussing or acting a fool you've seen splashed all over the news. A-list celebrities are known for that, and personally I think they do it on purpose (with the possible exception of singer/dancer Chris Brown or actor/director Mel Gibson, because even in the rarified world of celebrities, allegations of beating a woman simply are not cool).

It's not like it's really a surprise. Remember Rihanna's naked photos that she claimed were leaked? Come on, that's supposed to be a surprise? Her publicists probably were trying to promote some project or appearance or keep her name in the public eye. The same thing goes with Kanye West's naked photos, also "leaked." He actually rapped about sending photos of himself to some girl in a song—what are the chances of that being an accident?

When it comes to photos like this, most blogs will post them because they need the content and of course the hits that comes along with them. Concrete Loop doesn't, and for me it all comes down to a business decision. It could mess up my advertising dollars, and at the end of the day that's bad business for my brand.

Whenever you're contemplating using content that might be questionable, weigh it in light of how it might affect your advertising, as well as your traffic stats. You can't really separate the two—they are symbiotic.

Blogging etiquette, or netiquette

You've probably run across the term *netiquette* somewhere. It has to do with Internet etiquette. Here we're less concerned with how polite or correct you are on the net than how you interact with other bloggers and blogs. There are definite no-no's out there, and if you want to stay on good terms with your peers, you'll remember the "golden rules" of good blogging.

You might also see these rules in other parts of this book. That's because I believe you can't overdose on this stuff. If you violate basic blogging good behavior because you don't know better and then you learn the right way to do it and never go there again—well, that's one thing. But if you know you shouldn't and still turn bad behavior into a pattern, you're either going to end up in court or shunned by other bloggers, as well as readers and advertisers, or both.

Here are some blogging netiquette facts you should know:

- Steal photos and you'll go down in the blogging community (more on this in a future chapter). Think about it: this is no different from walking into a store, stuffing a shirt into your purse, then leaving without paying for it. When you post pictures that you found on my site—whether I have taken them or have paid someone else for them—without my permission, you are no better than a shoplifter. Doing this, even inadvertently, will be costly for you because it will get around the blogging community that you're a thief, and that will cost you readers, advertising, and community goodwill. Loyal readers of Concrete Loop e-mail me when they spot something on another blog. It's like having thousands and thousands of eyes looking out for us, which we really appreciate.
- Nothing is sacred on the Internet anymore, not even a blog's layout. New blogs are popping up all the time, and some of them take their inspiration from other, more established blogs. While it's okay to derive your inspiration from another blog, copying their looks or style is dishonest and will earn you a bad reputation. Think about

Lady Gaga, who has said she draws inspiration from Madonna. Lady Gaga doesn't copy Madonna, but does her own thing and takes it to a different level. Just like stealing photos and content, readers will know if you steal someone else's layout, so keep your hands in your pockets and develop your own unique style.

- Always give credit to your source and link back to posts whenever it's appropriate. By doing so, you not only give credit when you should, but you do the right thing, which benefits both you and the other blogger. Blogging is really competitive these days, and a lot of bloggers don't want to credit or link back because that could drive traffic to another blog, but if they use my material, I expect them to, and so do other bloggers. When I had a Pharrell Williams exclusive, other bloggers took my exclusive post and posted it to their own blogs without crediting me. And with Concrete Loop's Fifth Anniversary Relaunch party (there's an up close and personal look behind the scenes at the end of this book), even before the event I knew most of my "competition" wouldn't mention it. I had a bunch of celebrities there, so some photographers working for other blogs grabbed the photo ops and then posted the pictures, without saying where the celeb was snapped. I know that it's really competitive out there, but competition or not, you can't ignore the basic rules of good blogging, so *always give credit where credit is due.*

Some Dos and Don'ts You Need to Know

DON'T take someone's exclusive content or photos. DO ask permission first and give credit where it's due.

DON'T forget that the blogging world may be big, but readers know cheating when they see it. DO remember readers will out a dishonest blogger in a second.

DON'T grab someone else's layout or logo. DO use them for inspiration, but be original.

DON'T underestimate similar blogs. DO keep an eye out for ones that might have lifted something from your site.

DON'T forget to link back to other blogs. DO realize that good karma comes rolling back to you.

Angel's Sixth Law:
Go Forth and Google

In earlier chapters we talked about how the stereotypical blogger no longer rules the net. In fact, being a minority can work to your advantage when it comes to putting advertising bucks in your pockets. And that's not the only thing that's changed over the past few years.

Back in the day, minorities who tried to start businesses often found no one would take a chance on them. Banks rarely gave us business loans even if we could get our ventures off the ground, which meant we were often under-capitalized. Although loan money might be a little easier to come by now, the best news is that you don't need a lot of up-front cash to turn blogging into a money machine.

Because start-up costs for blogs are small, if you can drive even modest traffic to your blog, you can make money. By appealing to other minorities with saucy, relevant content, you can tap into an audience that other bloggers just don't get.

While it might sound counterintuitive to start slapping ads on your site at the beginning when your traffic is low, that's what I did. I put ads on Concrete Loop right from the start, and guess what? I started making money right away.

I'll admit it wasn't much at first, but eventually it all adds up. It took me a full eight to twelve months before I showed an appreciable profit. But there is a real, measurable side benefit to monetizing your blog early in the game, even though you may not be making a whole lot at first: You can track your growth from the very start. By watching your numbers, you can see what's working and what's not, which will better help you shape the direction of your blog, as well as its growth.

And it can grow a lot. Many bloggers make very respectable profits, even those who just blog on the side for a little extra income—I know one who rakes in about a grand a month from blog advertising. One well-known celebrity gossip-oriented blog brings in $111,000 a month (yes, that's *a month*) in advertising revenues. How do they make their blogs pay? The answer can be reduced to a four-word formula: They do it right. Read on and I'll show you how to duplicate their success without slogging through a mountain of trial and error.

First, let's look at the types of ads

At this stage in your career, Internet advertising probably elicits one of the following reactions: It annoys the crap out of you; it's so unobtrusive it might as well not be there; or it draws you in and makes you want to know more about the product or service advertised. (This one is the best reactions of all from the advertiser's—and blogger's—point of view.) This is especially true if the ad seems like it's directed specifically at you and your interests—that's the importance of matching your advertising to your blog. Bloggers who cater to minority audiences, like African Americans, need to gear their ad styles to that audience, something I'll talk more about later. For right now, I want you to cruise the web and take note of the various kinds of advertising, paying special attention to ads that catch your eye in a good way. Later, those will be your bread and butter.

Like anything geeky, web advertising has a language of its own. To make money with advertising on your blog, you need to know the difference between the types of ads and how they work. Here's a rundown on some of the basics (you can refresh your memory if you need to by checking out the glossary at the end of the book):

- Banner ad: A box with a hypertext link that, when clicked, will take the viewer to the advertiser's website. Banner ads come in differing sizes and may be animated.
- Banner exchange: Usually an organized network that allows websites to trade banners. You run my banner ad and I run yours—the network keeps track of how many visitors view them to let you know if the trade's working or not.

Banner ads can pay off in different ways, but these are the most common:

- CPCs: Cost per click, or click-throughs. A blogger is paid based on the number of people who click on the ad; please banish any thoughts you might have about clicking on your own ads. You can't make money that way. In the first place it's unethical, plus affiliate companies like Google Adsense (more about this a little later) recognize unique clicks.
- CPMs: Page views or impressions. Measured per thousand impressions. (By the way, M is the Roman numeral that stands for "thousand.")
- Pop-ups: Yep, those annoying as you-know-what boxes that pop onto your screen, sometimes making it impossible to continue what you're doing. Really prevalent with porn sites—there's even a virus associated with porn pop-ups known as the "no-close virus." There's

another variation called a pop-under, in which the ad actually appears beneath the web page so that you don't find it until you close your browser. Many browsers and antivirus software have developed the ability to block these ads, but ad companies keep finding ways to subvert the pop-up blockers.

- Interstitial ads: You know how you go to a web page and before you can access it, you have to look at an ad that's positioned either over the text or covers the whole page itself? Well, that's interstitial advertising in a nutshell. It's advertising that's in between pages.

- Contextual ads: The most common online advertising, contextual ads are targeted to the perceived interests of the viewer. It matches the ads up to whatever the viewer is looking at, like if you pull up the Concrete Loop photo of Janet Jackson looking hot in the front row of a fashion show with her stylist, you might find ads for clothes, accessories, hair care products and makeup, or even some of Janet's music on that page. There's also a second type of contextual ad called "in-text" ads. These ads appear in the actual editorial itself, but they're highlighted. If you click on them, they will link you to another site or open a box that contains advertising. For example, if you click on an in-text word like *rap* on Concrete Loop, it might take you to an ad for Jay-Z's newest release, or if you clicked on shoes, it could open up a box featuring Manolo Blahnik's latest designs.

- Takeover ads: These are big, well-produced, usually high-budget ads that literally "take over" a home page. Takeovers involve graphics, action, and usually some audio. They briefly overshadow the site's home page content. The goal of a takeover is to be spectacular enough for the viewer to want to watch it again. It's an ideal advertising choice for entertainment clients like mine.

Internet advertising itself can be further split into two different categories: ads sold by affiliate companies and ads you sell yourself. Let's take a look at the two types and what they offer to you and your blog.

Affiliate companies

The easiest and fastest way to launch the entrepreneurial side of your blog is to sign up for one or more of the ad affiliate programs. There are dozens of them out there, but I'll cover the ones I use and with which I have had the most success.

Affiliate programs work best if you understand how they operate and their rules right from the get-go. In order to integrate affiliate ads on your website, you need to be versed in ethical ad placement.

When I talk about ethics in this context, I don't mean your philosophical outlook. Instead, I'm referring to how your blog matches up with the affiliate company. For example, if you have a commercial site—say you have a site that sells jewelry—the affiliate won't partner with you. They want blogs with content, not one that simply pushes its own products and services. And again, you can't slip anything past them: They constantly review their partner sites and will yank your contract in a heartbeat if they catch you cheating.

Sites with no content or ones with mostly sales, pornography (except for ads that fit the interests of porn site users), and sites full of hate speech all get the thumbs-down from the affiliates with which I partner.

Here are the companies I recommend based on Concrete Loop's experiences. They're all user-friendly, have great support, and are set up to match you with the best advertising fits for your blog. I strongly recommend that you *do not* limit yourself to only one affiliate company; instead, partner with two or more. It will not only maximize your income, but also help you decide what companies are good fits for your site. If you look around, you'll find many affiliate ad companies have opened their doors, including one operated by Yahoo! Below you'll find the affiliate groups featured on Concrete Loop:

Google Adsense

Google Adsense was my first affiliate program, but the money I made in the beginning didn't exactly make me want to quit my day job. I think I made about two cents a day at the start, but like the old story about how to eat an elephant (by taking one bite at a time), you must tackle turning your blog into a moneymaker in baby steps. So, don't get discouraged if initial returns look like what's sitting in the Need-a-Penny, Take-a-Penny cups at the convenience store.

Enrolling in Google Adsense makes a lot of sense as it's easy to implement and the concept itself is simple. Let's take a closer look:

Q: How does Google Adsense work?

A: Google Adsense pays you to display ads on your site. These ads pay off in two ways, both of which we talked about before: CPC (cost per click) or CPM (cost per thousand impressions). Site visitors must actually click on the ad in order for you to get paid in the CPC model. In the CPM model, revenue is determined by how many visitors access a page. You don't have to choose one approach over the other: Google and the advertisers decide the CPC and CPM designations before they're placed.

Q: Can you really make money with an affiliate like Adsense?

A: Let's put it this way: Three weeks into September 2009, Concrete Loop had nine million impressions for Google Adsense. So, yeah, you can make money this way. In fact, Google Adsense is my biggest moneymaker. A lot of people like to knock them, but if you stick it through and optimize your blog (covered back in a previous chapter), you can go far. Like I said, the checks were small at first—the first one was $100. Take my word; they're a *lot* bigger now.

Q: What types of ads are we talking about?

A: The targeted kind. For example, Concrete Loop would have ads for books by African American writers, hot fashion accessories, or traditionally black universities. These ads are what is known as "contextually targeted"—they're matched to Concrete Loop's content. What we wouldn't have: Ads targeted to seniors, little children, or beauty aids that don't work for people of color. The ads and content complement one another, and that is one thing that makes Google Adsense work.

Q: What about ads from my competitors or stuff I find offensive?

A: Relax. Google is your friend. They want to give you money, but they're not trying to buy your soul. First off, Google doesn't approve hateful or pornographic advertisement. Same with ads from another web owner who keeps trying to rip off your content or a competing blogger—you can filter them out. You don't want to send your readers to your competition, not even if they pay you to do it. Also, you can also use their Ad Review Center to screen out placement targeted or contextual ads you don't want on your pages, although you can't just say, "No." You have to give Google a reason for not wanting them there.

Q: You mention making money off Google search too. How does that work?

A: Easy. Google search can help you make money in two ways. One is to have a Google search function right on your site. Visitors will type in what they want to search, say in this case it's "Beyoncé," and Google will search Concrete Loop for entries that mention Beyoncé. You can also set it up so that it searches other sites (no sweat with this—you choose the sites) or the entire web. Strictly your preference. That helps your traffic count, exposes visitors to the ads on those pages, and ups your chances of CPCs. This program's called Adsense for Search and it's free.

Q: And the second way?

A: Custom Search Engine (CSE) is the more advanced version offered by Adsense. It offers you more control and customization than Adsense for Search; for example, you can exclude sites from your searches or add words to searches your visitors initiate. CSE is a great tool, but I recommend learning your way around Adsense for Search and building your traffic before moving into CSE.

Q: How do the ads get on my site?

A: You put them there using basic HTML code copy and paste. Chances are you are already at least a little familiar with HTML, but if not, you must learn the basics. Google Adsense has a great tutorial on HTML and basic ad implementation. Check it out by going to Google Adsense "help," then clicking on the following in the order: Adsense help, Adding Adsense to my site, Ad implementation, and finally, Code Implementation Guide.

Q: How about the money? When do I get paid?

A: You'll start getting checks once your earnings reach your payment threshold. The threshold amount is determined by the type of currency you earn, such as British pounds or American dollars. If you're paid in dollars, then the threshold at the time this book was written is $100. Checks will come monthly if you regularly earn up to or beyond your threshold.

Q: How do I get paid?

A: Google offers a number of options, including checks and electronic funds transfers (EFT).

Q: Do I have to pay taxes the money I earn from Google?

A: Yes! It's all reportable income and Google complies with IRS guidelines.

Q: How do I get started?

A: First, go to www.google.com/adsense/. This will take you to a login page. Skip the login and scroll down to the bottom of the page where you will find a horizontal menu. Click on "help." This will display a large menu of options, as well as a search feature. I recommend reading through the information thoroughly and taking the tutorials before enrolling in Adsense, although it may seem like a huge amount of material at first. It's really not difficult once you learn the ropes, and Google wants you to succeed, so they offer tons of help. You can skip the stuff about HTML if you've already mastered that skill set.

Other affiliate companies

Google Adsense isn't the only ad program out there, but it's the biggest and most profitable. However, as huge corporations have learned, diversification is the key to maximizing profits. That's why I recommend you look into other ad programs as well. In addition to Google, here are the best of the rest:

- AdBrite: (www.adbrite.com) AdBrite is the tenth largest ad network on the web with over 110,000 affiliated sites, specializing in inexpensive options for advertisers. Among the types of ads offered by AdBrite are full-page interstitial ads. The pluses of working with

AdBrite are many: The company is well organized, offers a great variety of ads, and is very user-friendly with the bonus of being extremely intuitive in its setup. You can find out how to enroll in AdBrite's program by checking out their website.

- Kontera: (www.kontera.com) CPC modeled advertising with in-text delivery system. Kontera adds are customizable and blend well with the background content. Concrete Loop's visitors react very positively to Kontera's ads.
- AdGroups: (www.adgroups.com) Popular African American network that is very hands on. AdGroups sells large campaigns and is a target-based ad company. I've found AdGroups has a large selection of ads and it's a hardworking company with good support.

More about working with affiliate companies

The key to making affiliate ads work for you is all in how you interact with the company. You'll find that affiliate companies want you to succeed, but for the most part they are interested in an honest and open relationship—the same kind you want to have with your site's visitors. By following the affiliate's rules, you'll start and stay on the right foot.

For example, remember you can't build a good working relationship if you try to cheat on the clicks. Recruiting all of your friends to visit your site and click multiple times on the ads won't raise your revenue. Affiliate companies have software in place to keep track of stuff like this. If you're caught, they'll yank your participation in the program. It's not worth the risk.

Don't stop at affiliate advertising

Nothing says you can't sell your own advertising and there's a lot to recommend that you do so. On Concrete Loop, I have a contact form for those interested in advertising. They fill it out and I get right back to them. Advertising dollars can be hard to come by in lean times—never keep the customer waiting on you.

The rules of selling your own ads are a lot like working with the ad groups. Basically, remember that you want to match the ads to your content, but at the same time you don't want to subvert your personal morals and ethics by accepting advertising that goes against your beliefs. I don't want content I don't believe in, so ads for pornography or drug paraphernalia don't fly with me.

This is a good place to bring up trust, specifically the trust that you share with your readers. Say you have a blog about organic food. Would you run an ad for a major fast food chain? Or display an ad for baby formula on a site devoted to the art of breast-feeding? It's important to separate out the ads that conflict with your message and theme.

Since blogging is still in its infancy, the rules are still in the process of evolving. Recently, the Federal Communications Commission stepped into the fray to address what it considered a major advertising problem on blogs.

A few weeks before Christmas one year, a nationally known major box store chain was mentioned in hundreds of so-called mommy blogs across the Internet. Each blog contained a similar entry that mentioned specific products available at the store and asserted the items were all great deals. This wasn't some cosmic coincidence—the bloggers were paid to promote the products on their blogs, but integrated into the editorial as if it was real content, not as advertisements. In print this is called "advertorial."

Advertorials are generally marketed under a brand name—say a national real estate company like ReMax which puts out its own magazine—or are inserted into editorial pages in newspapers and magazines as if the stories are articles, but they are clearly marked as advertisements.

Up until now, the Internet has been a free-for-all, mixing advertisement with editorial in such a way that the lines have often appeared blurred to readers and bloggers alike. Now the FTC has jumped into the mix with a ruling that affects what some people call "blogger payola."

In October 2009, the FTC announced new guidelines that would require bloggers to disclose a material connection to an advertiser, which means both pay and freebies. This ruling covers the kinds of things mommy bloggers did with the big box product endorsements. You can find a press release with an overview of the ruling and additional information, including a link to the ruling itself, here: http://www.ftc.gov/opa/2009/10/endortest.shtm.

Ethically it's always been problematic for bloggers to accept money or other consideration in return for promotion disguised as editorial. Now it's also illegal. From here on out, bloggers have to disclose when they're getting paid or otherwise compensated—with free samples, music, tickets, or even trips—for their advertorials. Make sure you're always clear with your readers when you review something, especially if it's something you've been paid to promote.

Direct advertising

You understand how the affiliate companies work and have signed on with one or two or more. Now, you're ready to expand your horizons and put more ad revenue into your own pockets. Obviously, the best way to do that is to sell your own ads, but it's not like opening a lemonade stand. You can't simply produce the product, set a price, and sell it to people passing through. Instead you need to develop your business skills before you launch your own ads.

They're known as "direct advertising" and what they do is cut out the middleman. That means you keep more of the money your ads generate, but you also have to do more work to attract, price, and place them. You should approach these sales as if *you* are the affiliate company. Here are some questions you need to answer before you get started:

Q: Who is my target market?

A: This one's simple. Your target market for ads mirrors the market for your blog because it's one and the same. So your visitors will be the target of both content and advertising.

Q: How can I maximize ad revenue?

A: First, remember that more ads do not necessarily mean more money. It's the quality of the advertisers and their budgets that will determine how much you are paid for ads, and it's the amount and type of traffic your blog pulls in that determines your allure to advertisers. The best way to pump up your worth as an advertising venue is to pump up your reach as a blog. The more traffic you have, the more weight your word has, the more attention your blog draws, the more money you will make from the advertising on your site.

Q: I have enough traffic to sell a few ads. How do I figure out how much to charge?

A: This is where knowing your web stats and page impression statistics come in handy. When looking for websites to place ads, many companies will ask you about your monthly web hits and page views; basically they want to see your "rate card." A rate card is exactly what it sounds like: a list of what you charge for different types of ads on your site. They're what newspapers and magazines have been using for years, and the amounts fluctuate as the popularity of your site rises. If you are getting a lot of traffic, you can set higher rates. One way to determine how much to charge is to search for rate cards for similar blogs. Be sure to factor in traffic—the advertising game is all about the numbers. Having a rate card when trying to attract buyers to place ads shows you mean business. To see a typical rate card, search "example rate card" or check sites that sell advertising for their published rate cards.

Q: Does it matter where I place the ads?

A: Absolutely. And you can charge more for premium placement. First, remember that a lot of what you will learn about ads and ad placement is drawn from newspapers and magazines, which is exactly where the terms "above the fold" and "below the fold" originated. In newspapers, the fold was exactly that—the place where the paper folded over. Stories that appeared above the fold were usually the most important. On a web page, most of the content is not visible without scrolling down so the content that shows when you first pull up the page is considered "above the fold." The content—and advertising—there is worth more than what's below the fold because it's more likely to be read and seen by page visitors.

You can also place ads within or beside content, but when you do, make sure it's clear that it's not part of the content. You can wrap ads by putting a special border around them to distinguish them from content or place them between posts to set them apart. Ads placed to the sides and below the copy at the bottom of the page are also options, but no matter where you place the ads, remember that they should not overshadow or obscure your blog's content or pretty soon your visitors won't bother coming to your site anymore.

Q: What's a wrap-around ad?

A: A wrap-around ad is a blog post that is wrapped with advertisement. Say for example you feature fashion posts frequently on your blog and a prominent fashion company wants to promote an item, but since you don't do "advertorials," you offer them the wrap-around option. Most of these are consistent with blog comment and actually look great and blend in well if executed correctly.

Q: Could you explain what a full ad buyout is—and what kind of money we're talking about here?

A: A full buyout means an advertiser purchasing all possible ad spots on the blog, but mainly the above-the-fold ads and the main blog background. These ads are the moneymakers for most successful blogs and can bring in tens of thousands of dollars in just *one day*!

Q: What kinds of sites attract the most direct-placement advertising?

A: Entertainment sites—especially music-based sites. In fact, anything that's celebrity related and generates both a lot of page views and content.

Q: What can I do to make my site more ad friendly?

A: You definitely need to optimize your blog (SEO, remember?). Ad placement is key and learning to separate your content from banner ads will be better for you and your readers in the long run.

Q: How can I get advertisers to notice me?

A: Advertisers go for sites that are well put together and will blend with what they are advertising. I recommend a clean layout that will show the ads and your content in a positive light.

Q: I'm not really much of a salesperson. What about a few tips for selling my site?

A: Know your brand (and there's a whole lot more about that coming up). Since you are selling yourself and your website, you need to make sure you know exactly what you are and who reads your blog.

Q: What if I sell ads and they're not successful?

A: That's why you try a variety of ads and you experiment at first. Some are going to blend better with your content than others. Remember, when you first start out, it's all trial and error. Eventually you'll figure out what works best with your content and design and your sales will reflect that.

Q: Are there any ads I should simply avoid?

A: This is where your personal ethics come in. I make it a policy not to sell ads for anything I don't believe in. Remember, you develop a relationship with your readers based on trust. If they can't trust you—or the content you present, *and that includes ads*—you'll lose your readers. There's nothing readers hate worse than a sellout. I also stay away from personal ads. They don't pay much if they pay at all.

Adjusting your perspective

Advertising isn't simply about making money; it's also about blending it as seamlessly as possible into your web design. You want your ads to fit with the content, complement it, and form a whole that reflects where you want to go as a blogger. In order to keep your ads consistent with your blog and its platform, remember these crucial points:

- Walk in your visitors' shoes. Look at the ads as if you clicked onto a new website. Does the ad placement contribute to or detract from the page design? Is the color palette pleasing to the eye, or jarring? Is the page too busy, cluttered, or poorly arranged? If you look at your pages the way others do, you can make them better—and entice visitors to come back.
- Check your ad and content compatibility. Would you place ads for hunting products on a relationship blog? Pair an ad for edgy, modern home decor products on a blog that's all about preserving and restoring homes built in the early 1800s? Consider office product ads a great match for a foodie blog? No, no, and no.
- Consider the esthetics of your blog—this time we're talking layout and look. This is where you've got to eyeball each page: If ads interfere with the ability to read the content, are disproportionate, or throw off the page's balance, then you need to rethink what you're doing.
- No ads on your blog yet? You can still peep ads on other sites. Start at Concrete Loop and take a look at how my ads add to, not detract

from, the content. You'll see ads that are targeted to my readers, but the editorial content, not the ads, guide the pages. The ads are well placed, fit my overall color palette, and don't overwhelm the site. Still, I get maximum exposure from the target audience for my ad clients, which is why they buy from me.

Five quick takeaway tips

Running ads on a blog is a lot more than just popping the ads on the page and collecting checks. You have to approach it as a business because, after all, that's what it is. Before we move on to the next chapter, in which I share how to make money off your blog by building a brand, let's go back over a few key takeaway points:

1. Layout is key. Ad placement can define both your blog's look and your ability to sell ads.
2. More ads on the page won't necessarily translate to more income. In fact, too much on a page can actually lower ad values.
3. Your visitors expect honesty. And so do the affiliate programs and your advertisers. Give it to them.
4. Maximize success by matching your blog demographics to ad target demographics. You'll make your advertisers happy and you'll make more money.
5. Be patient. Lots of people see a blog and think that it doesn't look hard, so they give it a go. Then, when they don't make money right off the bat, they get discouraged. Blogging for money is a small-business program, and like any small business, it takes time to get off the ground.

Angel's Seventh Law:
Brand Your Blog

Love them or hate them, whatever you may think of the Kardashian family, they're geniuses at one very important modern media challenge: branding. Kim, the most visible and certainly the most notorious of the Kardashian sisters, first rocketed into the public eye when she was immortalized on a sex tape. Parlaying her indiscretion into a career, Kim became a media fixture along with her pal, Paris Hilton; both socialites and party girls without discernable talent or real jobs, that didn't stop either of them from becoming famous. Like Paris, Kim often was photographed leaving or arriving at clubs for a night of fun with her boyfriends (generally a mix of athletes and minor celebrities). Many in the media and entertainment world dismissed Kim and her clan as simply hangers-on or opportunists.

After parlaying their unusual family dynamics (their mom is married to former Olympian and present-day plastic-surgery addict Bruce Jenner) into a television show with its own spin-off (produced by *American Idol* and radio host Ryan Seacrest), Kim has branched out. Not only has she produced a show of her own, she's launched a perfume and clothing line and has entered the music business. She's also modeled for a number of world-renowned brands, and even been a contestant on *Dancing with the Stars* (for the record, she was booted early in the competition—while she can brand, the judges didn't think she could dance).

Still, Kim and her family are anything but empty-headed. They understand that branding is key to their ability to stay in the public eye and staying out front and visible keeps the money rolling in. Kim has also used her clout to transition her career into movies and "author" a book.

I'm not suggesting you "leak" a sex tape (and one thing those leaked tapes all have in common is that the people in them already have a degree of fame, so it wouldn't do you any good if you're not famous already), but branding— yourself and your blog— is essential if your blog is going to make any money or have any impact. You have to brand in order to develop staying power.

And that's the point. In the first part of my book I offered guidance in choosing your topic and naming your blog. I told you how to make creative choices that can both enhance your experience and set you up to turn a profit down the road. But now we're down to the things that will make or break your blogging, as well as turn your experiences into a career, as opposed to a hobby. Without a brand, you're just another web address. With a brand, you've got the potential to go all the way.

Why branding is important

When you think of branding, the first things that might pop into your mind are consumer products like Pepsi, Cheerios, or a hot designer like Vera Wang. Branding is no longer just for products or lines of clothing, though; it's also for individuals, blogs, and websites. Branding defines exactly who and what you and your blog really are: It reflects your identity, your personality, and ultimately the face you present to the world.

Concrete Loop's brand is something I guard like a pit bull. I know that anything I do under the name of Concrete Loop will reflect back on both the blog and my public, business self. Stepping outside of the context of the brand can change the perception people and advertisers can have of your blog. It's nothing to trifle with—establishing your brand is involved and time-consuming, and to get it right you'll have to think about every blog-related move you make. Then, you'll have to work twice as hard to keep it fresh, relevant, and at the top of its game.

Think of branding as the key to your corporate identity. It's a legitimate entity that individuals can relate to and, with luck, will recognize. Branding can take your blog to the next level by giving you a more professional standing. And branding stands for something—a certain level of quality—you can't brand yourself one way and then decide you want to change it and, with a snap of the fingers, just do it. It's much more complex than that—something you will understand by the time you reach the end of this chapter.

Branding opens a lot of doors for you: It can make you or your blog instantly recognizable. That has commercial value; companies pay a lot to associate with something or someone with the right branding. It can also pay off in advertising and promotional deals. Plus, if you brand yourself the right way, you can also translate your brand into merchandising and bigger deals down the road. Before this chapter's over, we'll explore the commercial side of branding and look at some of the ways you can parlay your brand into cashable opportunities, which expands your blog's potential for making money.

Two ways to brand your blog

When we talked about naming your blog, we looked at all of the reasons you might want to choose a unique, catchy name or, in the alternative, name your blog after yourself. Both have advantages, as well as disadvantages, when it comes to branding.

If you name your blog after yourself, you build in some long-term protection that keeps you associated with it. For instance, if you ever have a partnership deal and it blows up, they still have to incorporate you in it somehow because that's your name: You *are* the blog. You and your blog are irrevocably tied to each other. Think about a celebrity blog like the one Britney Spears has in connection to Buzz Media. Would www.BritneySpears.com be the same without Britney? Would it pull the same readership, have the same advertising punch, be the same product? Nope. And if your blog has your name or some form of your name, it's a lot harder to divorce you from it—which can be both good and bad.

It's also good to name your blog after yourself if you're looking to be famous and want to get your name out there. Selling yourself as a brand is one step closer to being on the red carpet—if that's your goal. I advise you to strongly weigh the pros and cons of moving into the public arena before you make that decision. We'll look more closely at that idea in a moment.

The other way is to pick a name and stand behind that name as a brand. In my opinion branding your blog name gives you more business leeway and the ability to branch out and do more with it. If you go with your own name, then, like I said, you're linked to it forever. Let's use my website as an example of how this works.

Concrete Loop has nothing to do with Angel Laws as a name, and since you already know the story behind choosing it, I won't go back over it here. But if one day I wanted to sell Concrete Loop, then I could walk away from it without any problems because it has an identity that doesn't depend on my presence. If I had named it Angel's Loop, then I would have to be there forever, because that's what Angel's Loop readers would recognize. The blog and the person would be indelibly connected, for good or bad, and I couldn't just up and divorce myself from it.

With a name that doesn't hold you up as a personal brand, there's a degree of separation. If you make it big with that type of brand (like I did with Concrete Loop), there's nothing to keep you from branching out and adding other sites. I did that with my personal blog, Angel on Fire.

I use Angel on Fire to promote myself, which also gives me two different income channels. The blogs play off each other and stir up cross-interest. Ultimately it comes down to this: Whatever avenue you choose has to work with your business goals and plans. (Don't worry if you don't have a business plan yet—I go over those at the end of the book.)

There are bloggers who have very popular blogs in their own names and they may one day have to face this issue if and when they decide to step away. And while it's great to contemplate having a "problem" of this caliber, in reality it's avoidable if you plan ahead. I'm a great believer in preplanning and anticipating future problems and in my opinion this is one issue you can sidestep by making the right decisions early on.

Professionalism in branding

Professionalism: That's the key when you're talking about branding. You'd better believe that advertisers who come to you and want to purchase ad space have already checked you out on Twitter and Facebook and have googled both you and your business. They've done their homework and have procured your stats. They already know how many page views you're pulling down and they understand your demographics. If they're knocking on your door, then your branding efforts are succeeding.

When branding comes to my mind, I automatically couple it with the word *legitimacy*. People know you for your service and/or your product. This is a reflection not simply of how good your end product is, but also of how well you brand it and how effective your blog is at getting its message across. And it reflects your professionalism.

A major component of Concrete Loop's brand is its positivity. We don't push the negative and get super-catty on the site. It's a conscious choice I've made. I want to associate Concrete Loop with interesting, accurate celebrity and industry news, not mudslinging and negative stuff that tears people down. That's one reason celebrities like Concrete Loop. We simply state the facts and let our readers make up their minds about the issues and talent we cover. And we aren't out for blood like so many of the other celebrity bloggers are. If Concrete Loop suddenly started roasting the celebs we cover, or being negative all of the time, we'd not only shift the readers' expectations of us, but we'd change how advertisers view us. Once you start becoming a brand, you also have to keep in mind all of the responsibilities that come with it.

And one of the responsibilities of your brand is that it must hold itself accountable for all of the content, even that left by site visitors in the comments area. This might come as a surprise because lots of people assume the blogger isn't responsible for comments left by others. While legally there might be some truth to that, bloggers bear a huge degree of accountability for their brand. You shouldn't tolerate comments that tarnish or go against the brand's image. That doesn't mean you shouldn't allow some spicy comments, even if your brand image is mom and dad and apple pie. Spicy can be good. Shaking things up can be good, but within reason; you need to keep an eye on those comments so they don't get out of hand. (I cover comments in more depth in a future chapter.) Right now you need to remember that managing the comments left on your blog allows you to interact personally with your readers, while at the same time representing your brand. In fact, everything you do once you start blogging should be an extension of branding your blog. Let me give you an example.

I give interviews to media outlets all of the time. This has been especially true over the past couple of years since Concrete Loop really took off. It's strange being on the other end of the microphone or camera, but if your blog's successful, enhanced contact with the media is one of the things you can expect to grow out of that success.

Interviewing celebrities has provided a real education for me. In the course of my job, I do a lot of interviews for Concrete Loop. Those interviews have helped me see the difference between a bad interview and a good one, which helps me when I have to give interviews. A bad interview not only makes the person being interviewed look stupid, full of himself, or uninteresting, but it can also affect the brand. When I speak for Concrete Loop, I have to keep in mind that I am always talking not just for me—even when the interview is supposedly not about Concrete Loop—but for my brand. As I said before, *everything* you do in front of or around other people will reflect on your brand. It's kind of like your reputation in high school. If you get a bad rep, you can't just live it down, especially in the online community. And that reputation is one of the many components advertisers will consider when deciding whether or not to spend money on your site.

As the founder and owner of your blog, you are ultimately responsible for any bad press you get and how that affects your bottom line. For some bloggers, having a negative image may be part of the game plan. Look at celebrity blogs where there's a lot of name-calling and pictures of celebs when they're a hot mess. Some people really like that negativity, and while I don't personally care for it, if that's what your brand is all about, then you'll approach your public relations from a different point of view than I will. But the overall point is the same: It's all about the blog all the time. And, oh yeah, the buck stops with you. It really does.

Perceptions

Speaking of negativity, how do you want your blog to be perceived? Reputable? Daring? Edgy? Squeaky-clean? Newsy? Gossipy? Whatever you build into your blog will be part of its brand, so deciding on your approach and material is more consequential than you may think.

Each post has the potential to change your brand. Think about that. Every time you add something to your blog, whether it's a feature or an advertisement or comments from others, you either add to or alter your brand. I'll show you how this works.

Let's say you've built a blog about shoes. You initially cover all types of shoes, from the kinds you buy at department stores to designer footwear. You include really good deals for name brand shoes that can be found in stores that specialize in buying manufacturers' overruns. Your brand then becomes a reliable source for finding good deals. You are successful and you experiment with other features. You add quality reviews where you look at the shoe and test it for types of materials and workmanship. You throw in a weekly poll and invite your readers to report where they've bought a to-die-for pair of shoes at a great price. You interview shoe designers and spotlight a little shoe history. Your information is solid, you keep the comments clean and in-line, and you stay up on shoe trends. What's your brand about?

- Smart shopping
- Solid product analysis
- Informative profiles
- Interesting historical tidbits
- Consumer opinions

Depending on how you approach the material, it can also be edgy, stylish, smart, authoritative, or all of the above. It all depends on you and how you present the material in your blog. Once again, everything you do on that blog contributes to or detracts from your brand. That is why all the things you put on your blog should be *consistent* with your brand.

Let's go back to your shoe site. You have successfully built a brand that is a reliable source for those in the market for shoes to use as a reference when researching their quality or price. There's also something there for the shoe enthusiast (and face it, who isn't?) who likes to read about shoes and her favorite designers. Additionally, you cater to the readers who like to have a little back and forth about the subject.

You have your tone and editorial philosophy down to a science and you realize that to keep readers interested and appeal to new ones, you need to change things up once in a while: Ditch less popular features, find jazzy new topics, and keep your boards supplied with plenty of stuff to talk about. So let's look at several approaches and how they can alter your brand:

1. You add a regular, interactive feature on celebrity footwear. Each day you feature a pair of shoes worn by a celeb and ask your readers to guess the designer —or the celeb. In the following day's post you provide the answer and perhaps a few more details about the shoes, such as how much they sell for or the materials they're made of.

Results: You've now added a celebrity component to your brand.

2. You go from a businesslike, straightforward editorial tone to something a little more gossipy. When you analyze the shoes on the market, you are snarky about shoes you don't like.

    Results: You've changed your tone and both advertisers and readers will notice. Some of your most loyal readers may not like it, but the new tone will probably result in new readers who will. The change will also up the snark quotient in your comments section. Depending on the extent of the snarkiness, designers may or may not want to be interviewed for profiles. Your brand is now less Oprah and more Howard Stern.

3. You add handbags into the mix, giving them the same treatment as the shoes you've been covering all this time.

    Results: You've expanded your brand. Now you must work hard to make your blog as authoritative about handbags as it is about shoes. You may or may not attract new advertisers: Handbag manufacturers are very likely to advertise on a site that covers shoes. If you add another retail product, say perfume, then you would probably also attract additional advertisers, since perfume is only tangentially related to shoes. You would also increase the amount of work and time involved in the site because now you have twice as much material with which to keep up.

Taking it to the mainstream

Most bloggers want to blog on the mainstream level because that's where the money is. Sure, you can make money with niche blogging, but your brand won't be as strong or as far-reaching. And most of the big advertising bucks are with the mainstream. It's a fact of blogging for money: Branding and advertising go hand in hand. If your branding says "niche," then that's the type of advertisers you'll reach. If you go mainstream, then you'll be more likely to attract advertisers that are shooting for larger markets. While Adidas may be interested in capturing the "eighteen- to twenty-year-old college student who is into playing dominoes" niche, most likely they aren't going to spend a lot of money grabbing a piece of that market. It's too narrow for them. Instead, they'll spend those bucks advertising on sites like Concrete Loop, with its broad appeal, or another blog like it that is also big enough to include those eighteen- to twenty-one-year-old domino fanatics.

This means you need to think like an advertiser in order to get the most advertising potential out of your blog. You brand in the direction of the money. Never forget when you're perfecting your brand that the ultimate goal is to be both accessible and attractive to advertisers. Otherwise you have a brand that is worth nothing.

Logos, colors, and themes

When you see that little Nike swoosh on an ad or item of apparel, you immediately know the company's name. That's how a logo works. Nike's swoosh was designed by a woman named Carolyn Davidson, who was a graphics student at the time. She reportedly based the swoosh on the shape of the wings on the Greek goddess of victory, whose name was, of course, Nike. That was back in 1971 and Davis was paid a whopping $35 for her design, although rumor has it Nike went back at a later date and gave her some swag to show their gratitude.

But the point here is that a logo doesn't have to be expensive or fancy to do the job. The swoosh is as simple a design as possible, yet it says everything the company needs it to say. While you might spend a lot more money coming up with something complicated or fancy, there's something to be said for simplicity, especially when that simplicity catches on. Let's look at a few other well-known logos and how they have worked.

Apple: Its logo says exactly what it is, an apple and the name of the company. It's simple, easy to understand, and impossible to mistake for something else. Apple's logo is an example of making an object work as a design.

McDonald's: Golden arches. Do I even need to say more?

Google: Pull up the main search page and you'll find the Google name in bright primary colors in easy-to-read Catull typeface. Google's design is known as a "logotype." Google occasionally loses that simple look and adopts a more complicated one for special occasions, like holidays and commemorations of special events or historic dates. Some say it's too simple, but its simplicity gives it versatility and that's why the logo works so well.

Starbucks: Use of the color green and the twin-tailed siren makes this logo stand out in any city street or airport (key for weary travelers trying to grab a cappuccino to stay awake for the next leg of their flights). While it's not a simple logo, it is instantly recognizable.

Chanel: The famous design house uses two *C*s, one forward and one backward, intertwined to note its corporate identity. It's beautiful and classically Chanel.

Playboy: Say what you want, but like Apple, you see the bunny, you think of the brand. It's one of those logos that needs no explanation.

Let's balance out the great with the not so great. Logos don't have to be design nightmares to be really bad. They just have to be forgettable. If no one remembers your logo, or they can't link the logo to the product, then it's a wash. Here a handful I think need do-overs:

Sears: Don't believe me? What's Sears' logo? Quick, no cheating. See? If you can't picture it, then it's probably not worth thinking about.

Alfa Romeo: Wouldn't turn down a free sample, but this baby is ugly. Lots of primary colors and a design that won't make Mercedes-Benz scrap its simple, signature look.

Playstation 3: With all that money, all that talent, and all that design capability, this logo takes simple to a whole new low. Plus, it just doesn't say "fun." Thumbs down.

Enron: Okay, I'll kick it when it's down. Including being synonymous with big corporate skullduggery, Enron had one wack corporate logo—a big angled *E* in primary colors that inspired zero confidence. Maybe everyone should have taken a cue from the ugly logo.

The Concrete Loop signature look

Concrete Loop has two logos. There is the CL that appears on the home page, which is a simple, easily recognizable logo. Like UPS, NBC, and other companies that use initials to identify themselves, the CL logo conveys to the reader an immediate sense of place. Plus it's a great, quick way to advertise Concrete Loop. That CL fits on just about anything, from hats to stickers. And since the design extends to the placement of the letters, it's more than just two letters stuck together: It's the logo as a whole that speaks for Concrete Loop.

But Concrete Loop also has another logo, and that's the one with the full website name on it. It's kind of like Donna Karan New York—she has both the

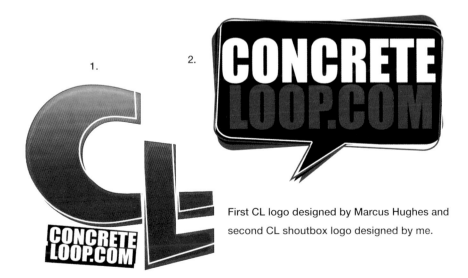

First CL logo designed by Marcus Hughes and second CL shoutbox logo designed by me.

full name of her company and DKNY. Both are the same brand; she simply has a full logo and a shorthand logo. Shorthand logos, like DKNY, fit a whole lot better on tags and even signature merchandise. Having a shortened version of your logo if you have a long name can help solidify your brand and give you a way to communicate quickly and precisely when you need to.

But we don't always use the shorthand version on everything. Concrete Loop is an interesting name (even if my brother, Justin, didn't think so at the beginning). It makes people who see it and don't know what it is ask questions. I can't tell you how many times I've sat in an airport with my Concrete Loop logo sticker on my laptop and had people ask what Concrete Loop is. I've met a lot of nice, interesting people this way and, who knows? Considering the number of businesspeople who travel, I might be catching the eye of potential advertisers.

That doesn't mean that everyone who sees the logo is unfamiliar with it. I also get approached by people who see it and say things like, "I thought it was you, but wasn't sure until I saw the Concrete Loop logo." Lots of travelers have told me how much they like Concrete Loop, which is totally cool. I also have T-shirts and other merchandise with Concrete Loop written on it and both I, and the CL team, wear them when we are out and about. It's extra advertising, stirs up public interest, and best of all—it's absolutely free, except for the cost of the merchandise.

This seems like a good place to mention your own future plans for merchandising because that, too, can turn into a revenue stream; in some cases the money from merchandising can rival the income you make from advertising, especially if you come up with something really catchy.

While you're considering logos and site design, take a moment to think ahead to when your blog catches on and becomes everyone's go-to blog for the kind of information and commentary you'll have. Do you want to sell T-shirts and hats? What about tote bags, jewelry, or something in line with your blog theme? For foodies this might be a line of cooking products with your blog's logo on it, or an apron, dish towels and pot holders. Maybe you'd like to develop your own line of spices or seasonings that fold neatly into your platform.

Fashionistas might look beyond the obvious promotional stuff like T-shirts to makeup products like lip gloss or even a fragrance line. While it's probably not something you're going to launch in a year or two, if you have it as a set goal, you can work towards it. Plan, plan, plan, and plan ahead. Do not let anything about your brand catch you by surprise. This, more than anything you do, will have the most lasting effect on your success and give you the most bang for your creative buck. Even if you don't sell merchandise and just use your blog name and logo for promotional products, you want your brand to be immediately identifiable when that logo is seen.

And remember, that logo and merchandise can be very, very useful when you do blog giveaways. Sure, you can solicit for giveaway items, but it's so nice and very professional to have your own stuff available too, especially for your blog's biggest fans. Don't discount the merchandise angle, even if you have no plans to go commercial with it. Having it on hand can come in handy in many ways you'll grow to appreciate as your blog's numbers climb.

If you're gifted in the graphic design department, you might be able to come up with something memorable and workable. If you're not, then go with something simple for now, and as soon as you can afford it, pay someone who knows what they are doing to design a logo for you. Shout out to Maryland-based graphic artist Marcus Hughes for designing the first CL logo. (I designed the second.)

Coloring your world

Let's talk about colors. No, you don't have to use the same colors all of the time, however, like your logo, if you want an integrated, immediately recognizable design, I'd suggest adding colors to your branding efforts.

The colors on your site are obviously not a substitute for good, solid copy; however, it's nice to be able to add another signature look to your blog. Here's what you get for your work: A style that's harder to rip off, a look that you can carry forward into your merchandising efforts, and a way to make your blog more "you."

"CL" uses a color combination that is all about Concrete Loop: pink and yellow. If you see a site in another color combo pretending to be us, then you've found a fake. Our brand identity is wrapped up in logo and colors—it's a visual thing. And we're proud of the way our colors impact our readers: They see them and they think, "Concrete Loop."

This is a good time to reinforce how important that kind of association is. Anything in branding that makes your brand stand out from the competition (in a good way, of course) is a leg up on the rest of the pack. If someone sees the "CL" logo, the Concrete Loop colors, or the other full logo and it makes her think of the site, it might also drive her to the site, which helps boost my blog's page views. That, in turn, drives advertisers to Concrete Loop. It's a win-win all the way around.

Not everything's a good idea

All branding is not created equal. Some ideas are better left unrealized. At least that's the conclusion I came to a few years back when I was talking to VH1 about a Concrete Loop television show.

The talks came about before VH1 was popping with reality shows—they have a reality show on everyone now—and someone came up with the idea that Concrete Loop might be a good taking-off point for a show. I attended a meeting with the VH1 people thinking it was an ordinary meeting, but it turned out to be a pitch meeting, so I told them about Concrete Loop and we talked about what a show based on my site would entail. At the end of the day, I didn't think that I was in the right spot to start doing a television show. For one thing, I didn't have my corporate papers filed; the laws involving television rights are pretty all-inclusive. They trademark everything. If I had gone with the reality show, especially at the beginning when the idea seemed so exciting, but I had none of the business end nailed down, who knows if I would still be involved with the site anymore?

Another incident involved a popular urban website that wanted to sign a partnership deal with Concrete Loop. They pretty much told me to name my price, and sign the dotted line. I was young, naive, and didn't know much about how corporations work, so I let my father and then later a lawyer read over the contract they sent. That was one of the smartest things I have ever done, and also one of the best arguments I can make for dropping the dollars on a lawyer who knows this business. If I had signed that contract, they would have more or less owned Concrete Loop and I would have been ousted after four years. Taken to its logical conclusion, I would not have done half of the stuff I've done with the blog. Who knows if it would still even be around?

Some notable celebs who were interested in working with or purchasing Concrete Loop included producer/businessman Jermaine Dupri and entrepreneurial giant Russell Simmons. I passed on both.

Even the big ones can fall

Some people have the magic touch when it comes to branding. Let's look at the Queen of Branding: Oprah. Face it, the woman is a branding genius. And one reason branding works for her is that she knows exactly what she is doing. Except for backing an occasional nutcase author's book, Oprah makes very few mistakes. And she understands exactly where her clout counts.

As I stated earlier in the book, her empire stretches from magazines to television to movies. It's almost exclusively entertainment and she understands the media inside and out. But one of her media giant rivals is seeing her own brand tank: Martha Stewart. Let's take a look at what's been happening with the domestic diva's brand lately.

At the end of 2010, Martha's flagship show's ratings on the Hallmark Channel were tanking. In fact, in its first month, reports revealed that Stewart's show drew fewer viewers than reruns of *The Golden Girls* when it held the same time slot. Another Martha product, a talk show featuring her daughter, Alexis, had even more abysmal ratings.

Ouch. Still, Martha Stewart isn't likely to end up around a burning trash can on some street corner. She still has plenty of lucrative deals going on, including partnerships with manufacturers and distributors, her own magazine, and her fingers in a lot of commercially successful pies. But the household authority seems to be losing steam, which is a bit of a surprise considering that her brand held pretty steady, even after she went to prison.

Martha isn't the only brand that suffered in 2010. Look at all of the sports figures who shot their brands in the foot with their bad behavior: Tiger Woods is probably the best known and most egregious of the athlete golden boys to go down the pike. And by damaging their brands, they also devalued them, which sent advertisers running for someone safer and more likely to bring in good press, not bad.

And that's good for the rest of us in a perverse way. When a star topples and falls, then the advertisers that desert that sinking ship are going to have to find another place to land. If we're lucky, they'll land on our decks and we can profit from other's mistakes. Still, it's always good to remember that just because you're hot one minute doesn't mean you'll be hot forever.

Ask almost any child star who didn't have a plan B.

Cobranding

If you're new to branding, then cobranding might be a new term for you, but as a concept, it's been around for a while. Cobranding is when two brands band together and cross-promote themselves or their products. Some cobranding results from companies reaching financial deals with others, like in a buyout, or when a product is linked to another through mutual goals. One good example of cobranding can be found on the set of *Project Runway*, the Heidi Klum show, which presents budding designers with a chance at the runway during New York's Fashion Week.

If you've watched *Project Runway*, one thing you'll certainly be familiar with is the array of companies that provide services to the show. During season 8, Garnier did the models' hair and their products were highlighted in the script. L'Oreal provided makeup and Mood provided the fabric for those fantastic (or not-so-hot) fashions. The accessories have been courtesy of Bluefly in past seasons, but were replaced in this one by Piperlime.

Bluefly has higher-end, more upscale accessories, and the thinking by bloggers at the time the change was announced was that Piperlime appealed to a younger demographic: Its look is trendier and its products less expensive, making its items more affordable to the average working girl, which is *Project Runway's* target audience.

But no matter what the reasoning behind the decision to partner with Piperlime over Bluefly, this is a great example of cobranding. And *Project Runway* cobrands with all of the corporate sponsors named, and at least one or two more I haven't named.

I like cobranding because it helps push a brand into territory where a brand on its own may not reach. By extending a brand's reach, you also extend its sales potential because advertisers look for the most bang for their advertising buck. So a chance to co-brand can be a win-win for everyone.

Concrete Loop had a great chance to experience cobranding when it became a media partner with Buzz Media. Buzz Media is a powerhouse in the entertainment blogging world, with numerous celebrity partners and some of the biggest entertainment blogs out there in their portfolio. As a result, they have a reach that's hard to beat.

When Buzz Media approached me about bringing Concrete Loop into its fold, a move that would involve a lot of cobranding and online cross-pollination, I had a lot to think about: How much control would I have to give up? Would I still determine the editorial direction Concrete Loop takes? Are the other Buzz Media blogs quality operations? Will the cobranding be good for my brand? And, obviously one of the most important considerations, will my readers and advertisers like the association?

After much back and forth, with my attorney vetting the contracts they offered, Buzz Media turned out to be the right direction for Concrete Loop. The cobranding with Buzz Media has been a success in numerous ways, and has already led to Concrete Loop's breaking new ground. In fact, in another example of cobranding that works, Buzz Media brought in Kodak to sponsor the Concrete Loop relaunch party (read the details in my party chapter).

Looking back at the kid who built a blog because she wanted something she couldn't find on the Internet, living in a small North Carolina town with not a whole lot to do, I have to admit that having an industry giant like Kodak find Concrete Loop attractive enough to partner with is a kick and a half. I never would have thought it would happen in million years. But then there are a lot of things I never thought would happen that did because of Concrete Loop and its reach.

If you partner with other bloggers and other brands, instead of working all by yourself, there's no telling what you can achieve. It extends your reach and your opportunity.

When you think of blogging, always consider the bigger picture, which is in the long run making money with major advertisers. You shouldn't diss the smaller advertising accounts, but your goal should be to bring in the big boys.

The Kodaks and the Diddys of this world will be able to spend more on your blog and money really does talk—because what it says is that you've arrived.

Brand identity

Your identity as a brand is uniquely you. It should reflect what your blog is all about, and point you in the direction you want to go. It should also give your readers what they want without compromising quality.

Celebrities who come to Concrete Loop know we use certain techniques that set us and our material apart from the crowd. For example, when we do candid shots, I do a little logo with Concrete Loop that's kind of a shoutbox. When I was backstage with Sway from MTV at the Kanye West tour, he saw all of the Concrete Loop stickers and said, "Oh yeah, I remember that. You do all of the 'Guess Who's.'"

He recognized Concrete Loop and I was pretty amazed at the time because it told me that he really does go to the site. It made me feel good, and it also illustrated the power of brand identity.

If there is a single most important concept that you need to master, this one is it: Develop a strong brand and you can have it all. Strong brand identity and recognition is what will make you money in the long run. It's what draws advertisers, what makes readers loyal to you, and what sets you apart from other sites that may cover some of the same geography as you do.

Don't dismiss branding as something you can put off until you have time. It should be an integral part of your blog right from the beginning. And the sooner you start developing a brand identity, the faster you can promote it.

It doesn't have to be complicated. You don't have to do it all at once or overnight and you can continue to develop your brand as you go along. However, the process of establishing your brand should be high on your list right from the beginning if you want to get your blog off to a running start and begin making money sooner rather than later.

Here are some things you should consider when putting together your brand:

1. Am I interested in becoming well-known because of my blog?
2. Could this blog be a stepping-stone to another career or blog?
3. How do I want this blog to be perceived?
4. What do I want this blog to stand for?
5. What quality controls will I build into this blog?
6. Do I want to build in merchandising potential?
7. What kind of a logo do I want?
8. What are my site's signature colors and look?
9. Will I associate certain features with my blog?
10. What can I do to make my brand stand out from others?

Angel's Eighth Law:
Work with Social Networks

Your blog is set up, you're excited, and ready to roll. Not so fast! If you're forgetting the role social media can play in your success, you're not looking at the whole picture.

Social media isn't just about updating your status and retweets. It isn't just for sharing photos of that concert you attended or keeping your family updated on your progress at school. It's a free and very valuable resource for growing your blog or business, and the more you know about how to work it, the faster you'll see results.

I've used social media networking since I started Concrete Loop, but as social media guru Christine Kirk of Social Muse Communications (www.socialmuse.com) says, no one is a social media expert because social media is always changing and growing. As long as it's still evolving, it is impossible to know everything there is to know about it.

PHOTO: Taj Washington

And that's what makes it so exciting. Blogging is one part of the whole picture. And while it's the main and most important part as far as you're concerned, you have to look at it as one component, not the whole enchilada. It's kind of like blogging is the main course of your meal and social media is the soup, salad, and dessert. It should

Diddy and I utilizing the social media platform Twitter during his album release party.

all fit together seamlessly and each piece of the social media puzzle should complement the others.

Although there are a lot of different types of social media out there, I am going to focus on the two that are most influential and important to Concrete Loop at this time: Twitter and Facebook. And, while other applications may come along that will supersede the power of these two social networking tools, right now they are the best the Internet has to offer.

Why you should use social networking

Think of the Internet as a big stage with millions of people all jockeying for attention. How are you going to stand out? Sure, being talented and putting together a great blog may get you noticed, but it's not always a ticket to making those big advertising dollars. In order to *get* attention, you have to *draw* attention to yourself. And that's one of the functions of social networking.

You also need to draw a line between your personal social networking and your blog's social networking. I deliberately separated Concrete Loop and its content from my personal life by setting up separate accounts on Twitter and Facebook to handle the stuff that I only want to share with friends and family. While I may share some personal stuff with Concrete Loop fans, they really aren't interested in the fact that I've had a long day and want a relaxing bubble bath. They want to know about the latest music, upcoming events, and if certain celebrities are as nice in person as they come across on television.

This is where I think a lot people make a big mistake with social media, including celebrities. They have a one-size-fits-all account, and as a result they don't look at how what they are sharing fits the format. For instance, lots of celebs have Twitter accounts and tons of followers. Their followers are fans that hope to broaden their personal connections with the celeb. Most celebrities don't have the time to sit down and read all of the comments and back-and-forth stuff posted by fans, but fans read everything the celeb posts. And what do a lot of celebs post? Sometimes it's a whole lot of self-promotion and not much else.

Yeah, yeah, I know. I said social media should be used as a promotional tool, but some celebrities take it overboard and common sense should tell them that's no way to treat their fans. If you're a celebrity, you need to break the rule of mixing business with pleasure and treat your fans to a look inside your world every once in a while. Plus, if you only use social media as a chance to promote, you're not going to build a fan base at all. If anything you will lose your current and potential readers' interest. I mean who wants to read incessant tweets about your new book, movie, or single? It's like a diet that features only one type of food—after a while it grows boring.

To be successful in the social media world, celebrities need to throw their fans a little love in the form of informal tweets, @replies, and posts every now and then. Don't get me wrong, I'm all for them promoting the release of their new movie, but at the same time, how about the occasional off-the-cuff stuff, the kind that makes a fan feel like an insider? If every post reeks of advertising, then fans won't feel at all special.

For bloggers though, the formula might be a little different. Christine Kirk suggests dividing the networking into four different increments, which is basically what I've done all along with Concrete Loop. It's a great way to spice up the promotional side of your blog with a little fan appreciation, while extending your reach into the communities you're tapping into for your readership and all it takes is a little math.

25 percent for bragging

Don't get me wrong, self-promoting is good. In fact, if you're planning on keeping your blog up and running, then you need to self-promote. You're in the business to stay in business and this is no time to be modest. So here is where you tell everyone about you, your upcoming projects, your blog, and anything else you want to brag on. Post those cool new photos and exclusives or drop hints about upcoming stories. This is where you put anything that might bring more readers and advertising to your site. If you sell products, you can also use this percentage of your social media network budget to spread the word. Have a branded tote bag that's on sale for $5? Tell people about it.

Just remember that like with the celebrities above, all this self-promoting can come off as self-indulgent, so keep this to 25 percent of your posts.

25 percent is for engaging with your audience

The difference between a dialogue and a soliloquy is that one involves exchanging remarks *with* other individuals while the other involves talking *to or at* others. Self-promotion is something you do to sell yourself and your work so that you can attract readers and bring your brand to the attention of advertisers. That said, most readers also want you to engage them in the conversation, not leave them out.

This 25 percent of your social networking budget should be a dialogue between you and your readers. Instead of sending them messages or putting up posts telling them what you're doing, converse with them. When someone asks a question, answer it. Say you have a food blog and someone tweets a question like "How long do you have to boil a shrimp for it to be cooked all the way through?" or "What is a roux?" Give them the answers if you can do it in a tweet, or if you have a recipe for roux on your site, post the link and guide them there. It's a win-win.

Engaging with readers lets them know you're not only paying attention to what they're saying, but you hear them, care about them, and that they're real live individuals to you. If you don't converse with your readers, you'll lose them. Everyone wants to be validated, to know they are important and that they count, and this is an excellent way to do precisely that. Answer tweets, respond to posts on your wall, or comment back on your blog. Never underestimate the thrill and rapport that comes from a shout-out like that. It's powerful stuff and the kind of thing that keeps your audience coming back to you for more.

25 percent for making things profitable, as well as fun

This is where you get the juices of your audience flowing by putting your money where your mouth is. Yes, we're talking about promotions, contests, and giveaways. They not only draw new readers, but also give your loyal following a chance to win some exclusive prizes. And don't think that small giveaways don't also score points in the reader loyalty department, because they do. In fact, readers who win even tiny promotions tend to stick around and become die-hard fans of your site.

What's that? You don't have anything of value to give away? Sure, you do. When I started Concrete Loop, I ran little contests all the time and, most of the time, financed the prizes right out of my own pocket. You can go to Best Buy and pick up a couple of CDs, or buy an inexpensive iTunes gift card for song downloads, and the winner will be thrilled. Or, give away your own promotional materials, like a T-shirt or hat with your blog's name on it. You're going to want to promote your brand anyway, so why not use this opportunity to start? Maybe it's not a trip to Paris or a chance to meet one of your favorite stars, but when you have a slim-to-nothing budget, you adjust.

And as your reputation as a blogger grows, you will start finding that opportunities to attract promotional merchandise and prizes from large companies will grow right along with you. For example, Concrete Loop held a look-alike contest for women resembling Kelly Rowland. We had an amazing number of entries and the kicker was so many of them really did look like her! It was unbelievable how many really great entries we had. The winner got some neat prizes, including a chance to meet Kelly herself.

That, of course, is the ultimate prize: the chance to meet a celebrity. It's also a prize that's out of reach for most bloggers, particularly those who are just starting out. So until you have the juice to get a celebrity to lend you a hand, find other ways to promote your contests.

25 percent for becoming an industry resource

While it goes against my grain to push one of my so-called competitors, sometimes it makes good business sense. One way you should look at this last 25 percent of your social networking time is that it's a way to make your brand an invaluable, indispensable resource and all it's going to cost you is a little time and effort.

Think of this as your *Miracle on 34th Street* percentage. Remember that old Christmas movie where the little girl didn't believe in Santa Claus and Macy's Department Store hired him as their store Santa? Remember what he did? He started sending shoppers to Macy's competitors when Macy's didn't have what they were looking for. At first, everyone thought him mad, but it turned out to be a terrific publicity stunt for the store. Macy's became the store with a heart. You don't have to go that far, but loosening up a little when it comes to your own industry really can accrue to your benefit.

For example, if you blog about fashion, then you want to become a source of good information on the fashion industry. You can do that by giving great industry-specific info to your followers. Say you have just left a Nicole Miller show at Fashion Week and her collection is heavy on miniskirts; let your followers know. Sure, you'll be doing some kind of follow-up on your blog, but right this minute, send them a tweet that "miniskirts will be huge in the spring!" You've given them up-to-date information before anyone else can, and in the process, you've established yourself as a resource on your industry.

It's not hard to become the go-to girl for industry news. You just have to work for it. If you're a food blogger and you have just found a fabulous new spice at a great price from an online company—share the news. You don't have to be in New York City or Los Angeles to be an informational resource.

Mommy bloggers can use their net time to point out resources that will make the lives of other moms easier and, in the process, pick up both good karma as well as advertisers. For instance, you can combine fashion and mommy blogging by talking about children's fashion—where do you buy hip clothes for the toddler crowd, what are the latest hot looks in kids' clothes, and tips on how to get the biggest bang for the buck. New York has some really upscale kiddie consignment shops. If you're in the city, check them out and report back on the bargains you find. If New York City is off your radar, check out ones that are close by. You do the legwork, talk about it, and it not only makes you authoritative, but also serves to enhance your brand.

And don't think that because you live in Podunk, USA, you can't be a resource for industry news. As you know, when I first started Concrete Loop, I covered celebrities and entertainment from a little town in North Carolina and everyone, from the celebs to their PR people, thought I was based either New York City or Los Angeles. You can position yourself to come up with great information even if you're not in the hub. You just have to pay attention and look for places where you can slide into the information void.

Using Christine Kirk's formula, you should be able to come up with a well-defined and balanced social networking strategy that maximizes its return for you. The key is to plan how you use social networking, not simply let it happen. If you are serious about the business aspects of blogging, then you have to treat social networking as an important and irreplaceable component of your business. Planning will only serve to maximize your chances of success; this is one area where hit or miss won't do the job.

All the little birdies go tweet, tweet, tweet

As I said, there are two main social networking platforms that I think shine above all the others and I'm going to talk about them individually. The first one is Twitter.

You probably already have a Twitter account and that's a good thing. Although various sources report differing numbers (and face it, due to the ever-shifting landscape of the Internet, which *is never* static, it's hard to pin down exact figures), estimates are that Twitter has more than 100 million accounts. According to the numbers crunchers between 250,000 and 400,000 new users flood Twitter each day. Twitter's requests number in the billions every single day. That's right—*billions*. Think of the bandwidth!

But just in case you are a shiny newbie and don't know how Twitter works, here's a short tutorial. (If you're a Twitter veteran, skip on to the next paragraph.)

Twitter (www.twitter.com) allows account holders to "tweet" short messages that are then sent to their followers. The messages cannot be more than 140 characters in length, and that includes spaces, but most of the time you can tweet as much you want (although if you tweet too much, your followers will probably all jump ship or you can even end up in twitter jail) and live links are allowed.

Your followers are people you know or who like what you're saying or, in the case of a blogger who is tweeting in connection with a brand, your readers. Personally, I think you need at least two Twitter accounts: one that's strictly personal and one that's blog related.

Unless you're a celebrity, your blog's readers aren't really interested in the bubble bath you plan to take in a few minutes or the wonderful sushi you had for dinner. In fact, if you blog about fashion and you're tweeting that you're mad at your BFF or it's raining and cold outside, you're probably going to get a lot of "what the you-know-what is she thinking?" reactions.

That's the kind of personal stuff you share with your friends and family. Don't make the mistake of thinking that since Twitter is short and sweet, it can also be short, sweet, and mundane. Mundane and your blog should not be on the same page. Save those "I'm bored" tweets for those who care. Your readers won't.

Twitter's a busy place and you need to punch it up to stand out. Make sure your blog's Twitter account is promoted on your site and put it into your e-mail signature. You're probably not going to have a lot of followers at first; that is something you build over time. In fact, the overwhelming majority of accounts (more than 95 percent by some estimates) have less than 100 followers. So don't despair if it takes a while to build a following on Twitter. This is a case of quality building quantity.

Here's some other interesting stuff from those who measure Twitter and its reach: Tweets reach their peak late at night (just before the midnight hour), so that means more people are on Twitter at that time. And the highest number of tweets are sent on Thursdays and Fridays. The most frequent users are women ages eighteen to thirty-four, which just happens to be Concrete Loop's demographics too.

Twitter has a lot going for it. It's popular, recognizable, and the short format allows users to stay in the know but doesn't drown them in information. It's the ideal format for communicating small bits of information with followers, like "Just saw Beyoncé coming out of XYZ restaurant" or "Exclusive interview with Solange Knowles on tap for tomorrow."

Remember, Twitter (and Facebook, too) aren't simply tools for communicating with your friends, they also help you build your following. Really savvy entertainers are using both to do exactly that. Some of the hottest Twitter accounts belong to celebs, and they not only post, but stir interest in their projects, support causes they believe in, and reveal a lot about their personalities and private lives through their use of social networking.

Here's a cross-section of what stars are tweeting as I work on this chapter: Ice-T posted a B. B. King quote, Paula Abdul is interacting with fans, one fan of Keri Hilson asked about an upcoming appearance she's making and got an answer, Diddy is plugging an app, Bill Cosby's making jokes about what he can't eat due to his age, and Tyrese is talking about one of his favorite entertainers. And those are just the first ones that pop up.

Twitter isn't just about the others who are on it; it's also a great way for you and your brand to stay relevant. Here's a good example: I like to tweet little tips to help novice bloggers navigate unknown blogging waters. One tip I tweeted was when you're traveling, you should start your draft early so that if you aren't at your computer, you can use your phone to post. I received lots of replies from bloggers who'd never thought of that. It's simple fundamental information that is both useful and qualifies as a resource for industry information (that fourth 25 percent, if you're keeping track).

If you want your tweets to reach as far as possible, you also need to learn to use hashtags (#). Make it your practice to search through top hashtags and employ them when tweeting. And when you have a great piece on your blog, create an appropriate hashtag to help spread the word.

Another idea for getting the most out of your Twitter experience is to search for tweets that are relevant to your topics and use the @reply feature to deliver answers to questions they've asked in the Twitterverse. By being useful, staying on topic, and coming up with replies to the questions potential readers are asking, you can invite them to your blog in a nice, oblique way. You're being helpful, not pushy, and you're adding a personal touch at the same time.

Retweeting is another way to steer news and information to your followers and also makes inroads with other Twitter users. By retweeting, you add to your own value without the heavy lifting of having to come up with original material. That doesn't mean you should retweet everything; stick to the stuff that your followers will find interesting. Funny or witty tweets should be at the top of your list.

I see Twitter as half of the must-have social networking for any blog; however, you must remember that the social networking book remains unfinished because it's constantly evolving. At the time I'm writing this, Twitter and Facebook rule. Who knows what will occupy the top slots a year from now?

Facebook: The other half of the equation

And that brings us to Facebook, the other 50 percent of what I consider to be the best of the best when it comes to using social networking to grow your blog and build your brand. As I stated before, I know there are lots of other social networking sites, and there will probably be even more around the corner. Who knows what the next wave of technology and design will bring? Until that wave hits the shore, though, I consider Twitter and Facebook to be the gold standards in getting your message out there and bringing readers—and advertisers—to your blog.

Facebook has more than half a billion users on it. No matter how you slice it, that's an incredible amount of reach. It's your job to see that your blog's Facebook page fits in with your brand. Your Facebook page should mirror your blog in terms of quality and coverage. Make sure your Facebook page is easily identifiable with your brand by making your logo your profile picture. You want to keep the visuals consistent—visitors should immediately know it's your blog.

Twitter and Facebook buttons should always be prominently displayed on every single post you make. You want readers to like your posts, retweet your tweets, and tell everyone they know about your blog. It's how you get the word out to potential readers and keep your own readership coming back for more.

Making your Facebook page fan friendly is all about surrounding your friends with things they know and love (your logo, skins, etc.) and giving them a reason to pop in and visit you. This is the place where you can add to your content by posting new videos or photos. Or you can tease the content on your blog by giving Facebook fans a little taste of what you've got on the blog: Post one or two pictures and link to your blog so they can see the rest.

It's also a great place to hold conversations with them: Ask their opinions about topics you cover on your blog, get their input on what they want to see from celebrities (or recipes if you're a foodie, or mommy tips if you're a mommy blogger), and use that intelligence to guide you in posting to your blog.

Facebook works as both a supplement to your blog and a way to stir up new interest and funnel traffic to it. Use it to your advantage.

I'll admit Concrete Loop has a long way to go as far as Facebook promotion goes, but the most important step is securing a page so that when you're ready to put in that hard work, you hit the ground running.

All the rest

I'm not into all of the types of social networking out there, but this isn't to say they won't work for you. If you like Foursquare and find a way to integrate it into your brand, then go for it. It wouldn't work for Concrete Loop, but say your blog is about shopping. I can see where Foursquare would fit your needs. However, if you're not careful, you can spend too much time on social networking for your blog and not enough on the blog itself. Remember—if the product isn't any good, then there's no point in drawing attention to it. It's like mounting a big advertising campaign for cookies that taste like cardboard: Everybody might know about them, but who is going to buy them twice? If you have quantity (lots of noise about your blog) without quality (great posts that make readers want to come back again and again to see what's up), your blog could sink like a cement block in a swimming pool.

I do think you can use YouTube to your advantage, especially if you're handy at making videos. These days it doesn't take a lot of expensive equipment to shoot something and post it. One of my favorite YouTube shows, *The Skorpion Show* (featuring Kevin Simmons and Makael McClendon), is a perfect example of using YouTube to your advantage on the celebrity end. If you have a food blog, you can record a cooking video and link it to your site. Are you a fashionista? Take your little HD Flip when you go shopping and show the world what's in and what's out (and yes, link it to your blog). I've seen people get popular on YouTube by just sitting there and talking. If you don't want to crop photos or put something together, you can just do a video blog. You never know when something will catch on and go viral and suddenly, you're the next big social networking star.

Flickr is another handy little tool that can help you raise the quality of your blog and what it has to offer. Post photos and then link them to your site and you can get traffic flowing both ways.

Flickr and YouTube are also ways to get around bandwidth limitations and still bring videos and photos to your readers. They're free and it won't cost you a cent, either for the opportunity or for the bandwidth.

Look at social networking as simply another tool in your moneymaking arsenal. Master it and you'll reap the rewards many times over.

Angel's Ninth Law:
Manage Your Comments, Know Your Liability

In the early days of Concrete Loop, I managed to tick off two A-listers: Tyra Banks and Diddy. Tyra threatened to sue me and Diddy gave me a piece of his mind. It was humbling in a way, empowering in another. In both cases, I came out fine because I understood the role of liability and how it works with a blog. When you finish this chapter, you will, too, but I want to point out right from the beginning that I am not a lawyer (and I don't play one on television). I can't give you legal advice and I am not going to try. What I will do is share my journey with you, tell you a few stories about how I operate Concrete Loop, and define some of the more important terms you're going to come across as you blog.

This is probably the single most important chapter in this book from the viewpoint that if you don't get what you can do on the web without incurring liability, then you run the risk of ending up in court on the other end of a lawsuit. That said, even if you do everything right, you can still get sued: Nobody can stop that, but if you have a solid basic understanding of what flies and what doesn't, you'll lessen the likelihood of being dragged into court. It is important to stay informed in this arena, and that means keeping up with relevant case law and the news.

My advice whenever you have a serious question about what you can and can't do on the web is to seek the opinion of an attorney, preferably one with experience in intellectual property rights. *There is no substitute for a good lawyer.* If you run into a situation that could have legal implications, then spring for the attorney's fee. Don't ask your friends, search it out on the net, or wing it, especially when it comes to things like contracts. You always want a lawyer to check out anything you sign and make good and sure you're not giving the farm away, so to speak.

That said, what can be said and done on the Internet is pretty wide open. In America, there's a little thing called freedom of speech. What you have to remember is that simply because you *can* say something it doesn't mean you *should*. That's where your ethics have to kick in.

Let's start off by looking at two of the most widely misunderstood aspects of writing: plagiarism and fair use.

Using someone else's work

If you have permission to reprint someone else's original work and they have the right to grant you reprint rights, then you have no problem. Remember, however, that unless they retain the rights to their own work, they can't give you permission to use it. That probably sounds confusing, so let's get more specific.

As a blogger or a writer, you automatically own what you produce unless you are working for someone else. One good example of how that works is if you are a newspaper reporter: The newspaper owns what you write for the paper as a staff writer because what you do is work for hire. They own the copyright unless you have a different arrangement, such as a syndicated column or the article comes from a wire service like the *Associated Press* (in which case you pay for the right to use it, but the *AP* keeps the copyright).

The same goes for writing that's produced after you've signed a contract for work for hire: Unless you have another specific arrangement with the publisher, you own your words and can grant others the right to reproduce them. That also means you can withhold the right to reproduce them, and if someone uses your words without permission, you have the right to ask for them to be taken down. We'll talk more about that in a bit.

Plagiarism is the unauthorized conversion of your words to benefit another. If you find a post on another person's blog that you like and you copy it and claim it's your own, then you've plagiarized content. If you lift a paragraph from a magazine article and put it on your blog under your byline, you've committed plagiarism. Anytime you incorporate someone else's work into your work substantially unchanged without giving them credit *and* while pretending you are the author, you have committed plagiarism. Plagiarism is particularly rampant on the Internet because a lot of people think that if it's posted somewhere, it's fair game. Sorry, no, it doesn't work that way.

What if you change things up and reword some of that lifted post? While you can use material written by others as the basis for research, if you also use an author's original writing, you must put it in quotes and attribute it to him. And this does not mean you can quote long passages. For instance, you can't take everything I've written for this chapter up to this point, put it in quotes and give me credit, and print it on your website. What you can do is quote a line or two, put those lines in quotes, give me credit, and say what the source material is (this book). Even better, quote a line or two, and offer a live link to www.ConcreteLoop.com, www.Amazon.com, www.BarnesandNoble.com, or some other bookseller where you can buy the book. That not only drives traffic to my site, but also could help sell a copy or two. If you do it the right way, you not only use my content legally, but you've made a friend in the process.

No matter how you dice it, plagiarism is never okay. If you plagiarize my work and pretend you created it, you're not only dishonest, you're also a thief. I don't know about you, but I guard my integrity and the integrity of what I post on Concrete Loop. Nothing is worth sullying it. Those who are too lazy to produce their own blog posts shouldn't be blogging at all.

It is inevitable that you are going to want to refer to the works of others. Even if you blog about nothing but your personal thoughts, you're going to find material you like and want to talk about. Since you have too much of a sense of honor to plagiarize, you must learn to incorporate the ideas of others in your work without stealing or claiming their work as your own.

Paraphrasing is a good way to do this. To paraphrase is to take another's work and put it in your own words. It's not simply rewriting what someone says, it's also interpreting it. Let's look at an example.

You read a news story written by Kelly Smith in *The Local Paper* with the following paragraph:

"Studies indicate that employees who suffer from clinical depression rarely use employee assistance programs put into place by their employers. They say they are afraid their bosses will find out about their depression and retaliate by firing them or reducing their responsibilities. As a result, most cases of job-related depression go untreated, which results in both in increased absenteeism, and increased presenteeism."

Since you blog about employment issues, you find this interesting and want to use it on your blog. You can ethically do it one of several ways:

1. Post a link: Reporter Kelly Smith wrote this piece about clinical depression at work for *The Local Paper* (insert live link).
2. Make a reference: Kelly Smith, writing for *The Local Paper*, says that presenteeism (showing up but doing little) and absenteeism (not showing up at all) are on the rise because workers aren't using their companies' employee assistance plans.
3. Use it as a pushing-off point for your own writing: Presenteeism is a new catchphrase for people who go to work, but might as well have stayed home. It describes the guy in the cubicle next to yours—you know, the one who has the basketball hoop over his trash can and spends his day making "baskets."

4. Quote the piece directly: According to *The Local Paper* staff writer Kelly Smith, "Most cases of job-related depression go untreated."

The plagiarism street runs both ways. You will find that people are also going to rip off your blog. It's inevitable and there's not much you can do to prevent it, but you can stay on top of it.

One really handy tool you can use to see if anyone has stolen your work is Copyscape (www.copyscape.com). Copyscape allows you to input your URL and then it will compare your material to what's out there on the Internet. The good thing about it is you can discover if others have used your work without paying you. The downside is that you only get ten free results; if you want more, you pay for the premium version. If you find your work is attracting a lot of unwanted attention from plagiarists, you might want to consider upgrading. It's a business expense and should be tax deductible if you're filing as a business.

Of course, finding that your work has been ripped off and actually doing anything about it are two separate things. I will give you a short primer on how to demand that your work be taken down at the end of this section, but first let's talk briefly about fair use.

Fair use

The concept known as "fair use" often is misunderstood by readers and bloggers. Fair use can be interpreted a ton of different ways and the courts stay busy with lawyers arguing all sides of the issue. The U.S. Copyright Office has a guide you can refer to that explains fair use: http://www.copyright.gov/fls/fl102.html. There is a link there that will take you to Title 17 of the U.S. Code, which goes into detail.

When it comes to invoking fair use, remember that it's not all black-and-white. Commentary, satire, reviews, material that is out of copyright or never was copyrighted, and other uses of someone else's work may be fair game under the law, but the law has nuances and simply plagiarizing another's work and calling it fair use shows both ignorance and a lack of character. My best advice, unless the work clearly falls under the definition of fair use, is to use a snippet of the work you cite and link to it. You can't ever go wrong that way.

Protected speech

Have you ever read a blog or blog comment and wondered how in the heck people can get away with saying the things they do? Well, sometimes they can't.

The Internet is still pretty new, and as a result, it's still evolving, and so are the laws that govern speech on the net. The United States has a very strong history of freedom of speech. We don't like to abridge another's speech without a really compelling reason. Protected speech often goes beyond speech that we like. It also can be speech that we don't like.

In this country people can say things that would put them in front of a firing squad in a dictatorial regime. The price we pay for our latitude in being able to say almost anything (and there are some serious exceptions to this that we'll talk about in a minute) is that we also have to put up with stuff that rubs us the wrong way. People can say ugly and hurtful things or stuff that goes against what you believe in because the First Amendment gives them that right and protects what they're saying.

While the First Amendment protects free speech, it also gives more latitude to talk about public figures than ordinary people. This is because a public figure has less of an expectation of privacy than your next-door neighbor. That's how all of those stories about celebrities cheating on their spouses or doing drugs end up in the tabloids. The press, even the sleazy publications, can get away with a lot more than you might think they should.

The U.S. Supreme Court has validated that Internet speech falls under the First Amendment; however acts that are illegal are not protected online anymore than they would be off-line.

If you have any doubts about what will fly and what won't, I suggest you dig into the Internet on a case-by-case basis and research what you're posting if you think it might be "iffy." Here's a good dissection of the First Amendment: http://www.law.umkc.edu/faculty/projects/ftrials/firstamendment/firstamendmenthome.htm.

Slander, Libel, and Defamation

This is where bloggers (especially celebrity bloggers) are going to get complaints: If you post something about someone and that person finds it offensive, you may be threatened with a civil action complaining that you have slandered the individual, which is what happened to me.

Back in June of 2007 (basically six months after I started Concrete Loop), I received a cease and desist letter from Tyra Banks's lawyers demanding that I take down a reference to a sex tape allegedly involving Tyra. The thing is Concrete Loop didn't run a story about a Tyra sex tape—another site did. Concrete Loop simply published a snippet of what the other site said and linked to it. There's nothing slanderous about linking to someone else's article or quoting another blogger or writer with attribution. Let me show you what I mean:

Right way: The 123XYZ blog today reported that Big Time Rapper had a hot affair with Another Big Time Rapper's wife. Here's the story (link). Or, you can do it this way: "Big Time Rapper is getting it on with Cheating Wife," reports 123XYZ blog.

Wrong way: Big Time Rapper is doing the nasty with Cheating Wife. They were seen checking out of The Expensive Hotel on Friday. Cheating Wife says the story is a lie and Big Time Rapper refused to comment.

In the first instance, you're attributing the information to someone else, which is also called "sourcing." You didn't say it. You repeated it and did it within the context of the original poster. In the second instance, you're taking the original poster's information and turning it into a fact. Since you don't have any evidence that the statement is true, other than the word of the original poster, you're on a lot shakier legal ground.

Of course, if you develop information from a reliable source and want to run with it, then it's your right to do so. If all the evidence points to your information being the truth, then you should be fine. One small caveat: Being right won't necessarily protect you against a frivolous lawsuit. Some people are just lawsuit happy and will threaten to sue you no matter what.

As far as the Tyra Banks incident is concerned, I used to be a big fan of hers, but that incident turned me off. Even more ridiculous is the fact that after hounding me about something someone else posted, Tyra had the blogger who originated the story she alleged was a lie on her show for an interview. So she ended up promoting the same blog that degraded her. Crazy, right? It made no sense to me.

The thing is, when it comes to public figures, you can get away with a little more than you can with regular joes. Celebrities, athletes, politicians, writers, and others (and this includes bloggers!) who are in the public eye have less of an expectation of privacy than the average person—guess it's the price of fame. There must be an element of malice involved in order to defame the public figure. Absent that malice, the courts have repeatedly exonerated news organizations; but to print something that the writer, editor, publisher, or blogger knows to be false will most likely constitute malice in the eyes of the court. So if you know a rumor or news item isn't true, the best option is to simply not go there.

The first time I had contact with Diddy was over a rumor I published involving him and Claudia Jordan, a model/TV personality and former beauty queen. She had posted some stuff on her MySpace (remember when that was popular?) that showed her sitting on Diddy's lap behind the scenes at some awards show. Not to mention, we also received an e-mail from a source that was there. So we asked in a rumor post if Diddy and Claudia were dating. I don't know how she did it, but Claudia got hold of my cell phone number and called me and said how much she loved Concrete Loop. Then she also asked if I'd remove the Concrete Loop comment about her and Diddy and told me that they were just good friends. She also sent me an e-mail about it. Naturally, I had a screen capture of the post already. I believe in documenting everything, which brings me to one really good piece of advice: Whenever you do a rumor post, make sure you document your sources because those are weird waters to walk on. In fact, Concrete Loop rarely does them anymore because it is simply not worth all the hassle and headaches.

Moving along with the story, I told Claudia that I would be happy to revise the post, but I guess she and Diddy managed to cross their wires because the next thing I knew Diddy was calling my parents' house—I still don't know how he got my parents' phone number—and he didn't bother to identify himself. Instead I picked up the receiver and heard a guy's voice say, "Who is this?" And I said, "Who is this? You called me." And we started cussing at each other. I had no idea who this guy was and why he was acting that way. Then he said, "You don't know anyone from Bad Boy? You don't know anyone from Sean John?" And I said, "Why would I know anyone from Bad Boy or Sean John? Who is this?" and then he said something that made me mad and I hung up the phone on him.

A few minutes later his assistant called me and told me that was Diddy and he was just upset about the Claudia Jordan post. And you know what? As soon as I had hung up the phone on him, I knew it was Diddy. I thought, "He was asking about Bad Boy . . ." and then I recognized his voice, but at the time it was so bizarre that it didn't hit me until after I hung up the phone. I told his assistant that we were going to edit the post and all was good, but our first real meeting was, shall we say, interesting?

I've had several run-ins with celebrities over posts. Let me tell you: They don't all want to be your friend! Not too long ago TV personality and singer Ray J and his lawyers tried to scare us about a post in which we gave our opinion about a video posted on another site. The warnings from his people were pretty unprofessional—they kept getting all kinds of stuff wrong. Plus, I'm a veteran of this game and know what I can and can't do and I can state my opinion on any subject I choose. You have to be careful, but you don't have to roll over every time someone tries to scare you. If you are meticulous about your content, do your due diligence, and keep copies of everything you won't have anything to worry about when it comes to proving your motives about a post.

Taking pictures

Pictures are pretty much the same as any other material you use on your site. Remember, they are copyrighted and the photographer owns the rights to his or her photos the same way a writer owns his or her words. These guys sell those rights just like we do. That's how photographers make their money and you should respect that. Plus you should respect that as a professional, intellectual property rights are both important and vital to our business. If you rip off a fellow blogger, then you're not only taking money away from that blogger, but you're also losing the respect of the blogging community. That loss of respect can go a long way towards changing your standing as a blogger. If no one trusts you and they find their stuff on your site, you're going to end up with a terrible reputation that's going to eventually reach the ears of your potential and current advertisers.

Lots of people don't think about photos as intellectual property, but I buy them all the time. Once I purchased a photo of one of the rappers from '90s group Kriss Kross when he was in the park looking rather disheveled. The photographer had offered it to a lot of sites, but I bought it and put it up on Concrete Loop. The next thing I know, another site had stolen it, cropped my logo, and provided no link back to my original story. I always put the Concrete Loop logo on photos we purchase exclusively, but thieves find ways around it. Just be aware that the same laws that apply to the theft of your writing also apply to image theft. If you find someone ripping off the photos you took or the photos you've bought, go after them the same way you'd pursue someone who stole your writing.

And here's the bottom line: I do everything I can think of to keep other fingers out of my pie. You'll find disclaimers on the site covering everything from photos to comments. You can take a look at them here: http://ConcreteLoop.com/disclaimer. You'll notice that they delineate my policies on unauthorized use of my intellectual property, as well as links and referrals (remember the Tyra Banks link?) and comments (which we'll get into in more depth in a moment). Depending on what kind of blogging you're doing, you will probably want to tailor your disclaimers to fit your circumstances—obviously a mommy blogger won't need a policy on music reviews and downloads. Your best bet—I will say it again—*shell out for a good lawyer!* Once again, there are some things you should never stint on and quality legal advice is one of them.

Comments and moderation

Your first decision in this arena will be whether or not to allow comments. I think comments are important: They allow readers to be a part of the blog, offer extremely valuable feedback, and allow advertisers see visible evidence of reader interest. However, while there's no denying that the comments section of any blog is going to be a lot of work for the blogger, the potential benefits outweigh that factor.

Comments Sections

1. Let you speak directly with your readers.
2. Measure the popularity of posts.
3. Hear the opinions of readers in regards to posts.

Comments sections should always have ground rules. It's the no-holds-barred part of your blog, kind of like the wild, wild West. I strongly advise you to set up your ground rules before negativity sets in and takes over your blog. I also recommend that your write down those ground rules for your readers and adhere to them as you build your blog. You can always go back from time to time and review to see what works and what doesn't. Below are my recommendations for basic ground rules:

1. Outline what can and cannot be said in the comments area, including racist remarks, gender bashing, and unnecessary hatred towards you and your readers. Tell readers whether or not you will allow them to promote their own blogs. Usually when people see you getting a fair amount of comments, they want to start promoting their own blogs. I don't have a problem with it if it's done respectfully. Don't go around saying, "This blog is wack, check out mine at www.betterthanthisblog.com." Or, "This blog is boring. I wrote the same story over at www.betterthanthisblog.com." That's a turnoff to the blog owner and will definitely get you on the banned list. Staying on topic: If the blog post is about the best pizza restaurant, the individuals commenting should say what their fave pizza restaurants are. They can add a plug for their own blog at the bottom, but they shouldn't use the post only to promote themselves or their blog.

2. Moderate, moderate, moderate. Some blogs don't care who comments as long as there *are* comments. They don't moderate or edit out anything. I personally feel that this is the messy approach to blogging, and when a visitor is reading through your comments, it can become a battlefield of derogatory terms and miscellaneous advertisements instead of actual feedback on a certain subject. This is a personal turnoff for me and most likely to many of your visitors as well. I recommend putting the backend of your blog to good use. My favorite blogging platform, WordPress, has excellent moderating options, including the "moderation queue" and the "comment blacklist."

3. Cut out the SPAM. Persistent problems for many blogs are the spam bots and their comments. They come back again and again, promoting everything from dating websites to laundry detergents. There are many ways to cut down on them, including adding their names to your website's comment banned list—so all of their comments are blocked or have to be approved—or banning their IP addresses so they can't come back.

Speaking of which, don't forget that the comments section of your blog can be a big moneymaker for you. Advertisers get to see what your core audience thinks and what subjects they're interested in; and, you can add advertisements above the comment box so they are easily visible (make that "impossible to miss") to the reader.

More feedback shouldn't be your motivator: Good content should. If you blog and blog well, they will come.

A few words about comments and liability

I'll say it again: I am not a lawyer and most of what I know about blogging and the legal issues surrounding blogging comes from experience and having a really good intellectual properties attorney on retainer. So nothing I am going to tell you about liability is legal advice. It's simply a summation of my experience and what I know from dealing with other bloggers. If you have a legal issue, go to a lawyer—don't try and work it out yourself, especially if you think it could lead to some problems down the road.

That said, you must also remember that the Internet is constantly changing and so are the rules and regulations surrounding use of the web. What is true right this minute might not hold next week or month. It's up to you to stay on top of things.

Another important concept you must keep in mind is that what is clearly allowed under U.S. law may be illegal in another country. Our degree of tolerance and protection of free speech is greatly different than what countries like China or Laos might allow. Even Westernized countries may have different laws surrounding libel and slander than we do, so keep in mind that while our laws may prevent you from being dragged into court here in this country, they may not protect you in another.

And that brings us to the liability you can incur when it comes to comments. A few years ago a woman started a site called www.dontdatehimgirl.com. The site allows women to post photos and (mostly derogatory) stories about men they have dated. The site grew immensely popular (with women—men were another story). Then an attorney sued the site for comments posted about him. He also said he would sue a couple of the women who posted the remarks, which he claimed were untrue. I don't know if he ever followed up on those threats to sue the women who were posting, but the courts in two states have dismissed his lawsuits against the site owner. In general, it is accepted that the site owner is not responsible for the remarks made by others in the comments section. While it's good to know, remember that doesn't mean someone can't sue you anyway. It just means that they are just means that they are unlikely to succeed based on present case law. And present case law could change Just. Like. That.

A final tool for you

If you find that someone has ripped off your post or photograph, or if for any reason you need to locate the owner of a website, there are ways to find out. Whois.net is a free service (most of the time) that will give you the owner information for a domain. You can find the street addresses, phone numbers, and e-mails of the owners and webmasters and contact them directly.

Also, when you demand that someone take down your material, in most cases they have twenty-four to forty-eight hours to comply with that request. Give them that time and you'll find that most people will go ahead and remove the item. If they don't, then the next step is to contact their Internet service provider (ISP). The ISP will usually ask the client to take down the material. If they don't, the ISP can shut down the site. A final step before you go to a lawyer and start action is to consider using a service that enforces the Digital Millennium Copyright Act, which will go to bat on your behalf—for a fee. And that means you need to decide whether it's worth the money before you go the distance.

Ultimately, you will find that there are people out there who do not respect your rights to your own intellectual property or the stuff you've purchased. They are going to try and steal it. It's a constant, never-ending battle, and one you're going to wage every single moment of your blogging career. Arm yourself with knowledge and remain vigilant. You are your own best advocate in these situations.

Angel Dishes:
The Ins and Outs of Celebrity Blogging

L et me let you in on a little secret: the life of a popular celebrity blogger is nothing but nonstop glamour. You spend all of your time hanging out with the "beautiful people," going to parties, eating the finest food, drinking the best liquors, and mingling with great minds and talent. You fall into your bed after partying all night, spend your afternoons gossiping about the business with record and music company moguls, and spend hours trying to decide what you are going to do with all of the swag big companies send you to curry favor. You are so busy sorting through invitations to A-list events you hardly have time to go for those free spa days and fashion show invitations with which you're constantly bombarded.

Yeah, the life of a popular celebrity blogger is one of 24/7 glamour, excitement, and partying. And if that's what you want out of blogging, I strongly suggest you find something else about which to blog.

Do you want the naked, unvarnished truth? Well, I'm here to give it to you. Sure, successful celebrity bloggers get to meet the rich and famous, receive invitations to A-list events, and cover private parties thrown by the people who grace the cover of *People*, but the glamour is *all theirs*. Their jobs are to be entertainers, entertainment executives, high-rolling entrepreneurs, and celebrities. Your job is to cover what they do. When you do attend an event, you're not sipping from champagne flutes and scooping up caviar (or at least you shouldn't be if you're doing your job); you are working. You are taking pictures, interviewing people, taking notes, and making sure you get as much as possible out of the event because you have a job to do. And when you finally get to go home, you don't crawl in bed and sleep in the next morning because you had a late night. You go to work on those blog posts, cropping those pictures, making sure your scoops get on your blog before anyone else's. In a nutshell: Sometimes blogging about celebrities is as glamorous as working in a car wash. The people are more famous, but it's still hard and time-consuming work.

In my office in New York City.

Don't get me wrong, that doesn't mean I don't love what I do. I'd never say that. There are lots of perks that come with celebrity blogging if you hang in and establish yourself, but I don't want you to think that celebrity blogging is all about "you" living the life of a celebrity. It's not, anymore than being a celebrity's personal assistant is being a celebrity. Anyone who blogs about celebrities who thinks it's easy peasy isn't doing the job right. If you want to be on top in this business, it takes hard work, long hours, a lot of research, commitment, and a very thick skin to get there. You can't be a party animal and still meet the needs of your readers. Plus it's important to remember that even when you finally get to the point where you are receiving invitations to events and parties, you're being invited as a member of the press—not as a buddy, pal, or guest. *It's your job.*

In this chapter I am going to try and shed a little light on what the job of celebrity blogger is really like, how you can blog about celebrities even if you're in Missouri or Alabama, and strategies to help you build a successful celebrity blog with little money, and no trips to New York City or Los Angeles. By the time I'm finished with you, you will find that the scant resources you think you have can be stretched, and you'll discover new resources for material appropriate for your blog all around you. Ready to learn how to dish about your favorite stars? Let's get busy.

Location, location, and location—it doesn't count

Location might be vital when you're selling a house, but when it comes to celebrity blogging, it doesn't matter where you are. I take that back: When you hit a certain level, it helps to have a presence in a big entertainment-centric city, but it's not a deal-killer to start or even continue your blogging in Albuquerque or Des Moines, or even a town so small it doesn't have a McDonald's. The key is to know where to find what you need to pump up that blog.

As I said before, I started Concrete Loop in Jacksonville, North Carolina, which is a small- to medium-sized town outside the large Marine Corps base of Camp Lejeune. (In fact, when I moved to Manhattan in July 2010, everyone I ran into at events and appearances already thought I lived there. As I told you in an earlier chapter, you can make a good chunk of change while living miles from the main action—I am living proof of that.) No one, least of all the people who live there, will pretend that it's an entertainment mecca (although a curious number of celebrities have connections to the place, including singer-songwriter Ryan Adams, who is from Jacksonville, and whose family lives not far from mine). Jacksonville isn't even easy to get to—it's on the coast with a nice stretch of beach a few miles away from the city limits, but the locals always say, "You can't get there from here." And they're right: Jacksonville is on U.S. 17, the so-called Ocean Highway, but it's not on an interstate or even close to one. You only get to Jacksonville if you're going to Jacksonville.

So how did someone living in a place that isn't even within hailing distance of a major modern thoroughfare manage to fill page after page of a blog with the names and images of world-class celebrities without leaving home? The answer: I taught myself how to find the material. Here's how.

Finding stories

It's not that hard. Really. While it may seem like a real stretch to cover the red carpet when you've never even seen one up close, you can find tons of information right at your fingertips and come up with your own unique take on the subject. You must, however, remember what I said about liability in the previous chapter: You can't reprint material you find on the web unless the owner/originator gives you express permission to do so. This is where finding stories and linking to them will fill your blog's pages.

Most news outlets *like* for bloggers to link to their material. www.CNN.com is particularly good about this and they have plenty of celeb coverage. The trick is to write an original couple of sentences that introduce the story (or use block quotes to set off something from the original story), and then offer a link for your readers. This ramps up the traffic on the original site and gives your readers a convenient way to find lots of material without having to cruise the net for it.

Think of it as being a train engineer, guiding the train through stops at various stations. You open the doors and let people on and off. That's essentially what you're doing here: Providing a vehicle to get them where they want to go, or in this case, to get them the news and gossip they want. Plus, if you're simply pointing them to the content on other websites, you limit your liability. As I mentioned earlier, liability is a very big issue in celebrity blogging, but we'll talk about the specifics there later.

In the past some news sources, like the *Associated Press*, adopted pretty stringent rules concerning how much of their copy you can use before they charge you for it. Be sure and know what the parameters are before you're tempted to just grab the first couple of lines and link to it. Sometimes the best policy is to write the introduction in your own words. That doesn't mean rearranging the words of the original story, it means putting your own unique spin on them. Let's look at an example:

MTV ran a short gossipy item linking Fabolous to Amber Rose, the ex–Ford model who appeared in his video, "You Be Killin' 'Em." Fabolous denied any relationship with Rose. Without using the MTV copy as anything but source material, you can come up with two sentences to tease the story and put in a hot link. The MTV story didn't contain a picture of Rose, although it did offer a link to the video clip. You can spice up your own blog post by adding the missing element: a picture of Rose (more about how to find and legally use photos later on). Or you can use block quotes and then link your post to MTVs.

In other entertainment news that broke at the same time the Fabolous/ Rose story appeared, there were articles about Mary J. Blige's upcoming album, stories about how some reality shows were featuring the girlfriends of hip-hop artists, announcements about plans for Kanye West to produce singing sensation Justin Beiber, accounts and photos of celebs attending sporting events, and lots more. In fact, there is enough material in one day for dozens of posts, depending on your focus, needs, and time. Using block quotes and links the right way will let you legitimately add material to your site without stepping on anyone's toes.

This is a good place to open the discussion on rumor posts. They are really a liability catchall and an easy way to end up in court, even if you're really, really careful. I choose not to post that many anymore (I think they're more trouble than they are worth, frankly), but you might want to, and that's fine. A lot of big celebrity blogs have made their mark by running rumor posts. If you do use rumors, you need to make sure you word those posts very, very carefully: Use "allegedly" and "reportedly" and make your sourcing material clear. Let me give you an example.

You find a rumor on another blog that Rapper A is having an affair with Rapper B's girlfriend, "Miss C." If I were running that item, I'd say, "Blog D alleges Miss C is spending a lot of time with Rapper A." Then I'd add the link. I've protected myself three ways here: (1) I've attributed the material to the original source, (2) couched the material in a phrase that indicates it's a rumor (alleges), and (3) pointed readers to that source so they can read it for themselves. Am I being overly cautious? Nope. Here's why.

Celebrity blogging attracts legal threats

In the last chapter I talked a lot about liability and how to protect your-self from incurring it, but one thing you need to always remember while blogging is that *being right won't keep people from suing you.* America is a litigation-happy country, and even if you do everything by the book, as a celebrity blogger you are going to get your fair share of communications from high-powered lawyers threatening to take you to court.

I'm not trying to scare you off, I'm just telling you like it is. I have received plenty of e-mails and letters from the representatives of public figures threatening me with legal action, and so have other celebrity bloggers. Celebrities are the worst of the worst when it comes to threatening legal action. Most other blogging categories don't have the same level of risk. Think about it: Who is going to threaten a mommy blogger with a lawsuit? Celebrities have teams of people on retainer whose job it is to look after the celebrity's interests; they also have all the money in the world to pursue a legal action and they're powerful people. Even if you dot your i's and cross your t's, you will hear from lawyers if you blog about celebrities. It's the nature of the business.

How do some celeb blogs and sites get away with publishing the stuff they do? Some have lawyers or teams of lawyers working for them. Harvey Levin, managing editor of TMZ, is an attorney. He polices everything TMZ publishes, but even with a lawyer on board, TMZ has been sued in the past. It's simply not possible to prevent all lawsuits, especially when you're writing about celebs all the time, but it is entirely possible to limit the damages and extent of any legal action by doing your homework.

Celebrity blogging comes with some special baggage and you need to know that while it has a lot in common with other types of blogging, it also carries its own unique set of pitfalls. Being extra scrupulous about what you post can help limit the opportunities for legal action.

And at the risk of sounding like a broken record (I can't emphasize this enough): Wording is absolutely key here, especially when you're publishing rumors. If you slip and leave out the "alleged" or "reported" part of a post and print it as if it's a fact, they will nail you.

Photo companies

If you post photos that you don't have a right to and the photo company finds out about it, you better believe you are going to get an invoice. It's amazing how much some of these photos cost—think $800 for one picture! However, you can find lots of free or very cheap celebrity photos for your blog on the net.

The very best way for an unknown up-and-coming blogger to secure good photos is to go the old-fashioned route (one that a lot of bloggers don't do as much as they used to) and team up with other fan or celebrity blogs and share photos.

For example, if someone asks Concrete Loop if they can use one of my photos, I'll almost always let them as long as they leave my logo on the picture (which shows where it came from) and they link back to me. Remember never to crop out the source blog's logo. If you do, that's no different from stealing from the source. When you do use my photos and give me proper attribution, it ends up as great promotion that helps both of us. I don't know why bloggers don't form these kinds of relationships with other bloggers as much as they used to. Both blogs profit from these symbiotic arrangements.

For example, Oh No They Didn't (http://community.livejournal.com/ohnotheydidnt/), which is also part of Buzz Media, has lots of photos posted that you can use if you do it the way I explained above. Another good resource for photographs can be the photographers themselves. Http://Meetthefamous.com is a great website that allows photographers to upload their own photos. You can find pictures of almost any celebrity on this site, with images taken by people who encounter someone well-known to members of the paparazzi. You can buy photos directly from the site—some are as cheap as $10 (and they may even be cheaper if the photos aren't exclusives).

You can also try tracking down photographers yourself and purchasing photos directly from them. Who knows? You might be able to get an even better deal by dealing directly with the photographer, especially if you make sure you offer him prominent credit. Everyone likes to be known for his or her work.

News organizations buy photos all the time, and some of the best come from the average guy out there on the street, who just happened to have a camera handy when someone famous strolled by. Who says you can't get star photos if you live on a farm in the Midwest? Not me. Remember—I had pictures of famous people all over Concrete Loop and I lived light years away from the action.

When Angel dresses up

Time for a little story that might make you smile. Like anybody who is embarking on something new, I struggled at first, but it didn't take very long for Concrete Loop to take off. When it did blow up, I was honored to be recognized for my efforts. Sometimes this recognition was, in retrospect, not such a hot thing. Or at least my reaction to it wasn't.

Let me explain. Back in 2007, *Radar Magazine* (which is now online only) honored what they termed the "New Radicals," and featured a list of up-and-coming bloggers in the mag. They threw an exclusive gala in New York City in celebration of the issue. I received the invitation while living with my parents back in Jacksonville and, since I never had been to a "gala,"

I figured it was a dressy event. Not to mention, I spoke to various people setting up the event and was told it would be. Little did I know, it wasn't.

I went out and bought a fancy, formal dress. It was a gold lame ball gown and very Hollywood. I topped the outfit off with a terrible wig—kind of like the cherry on top of the sundae. (In my defense, I didn't really want to wear the wig but someone told me it looked good. It didn't.) The whole look cost me a fortune, but I didn't care. It was one of the most exciting moments of my life up until then. Of course, as it turned out, it would actually end up being one of the most embarrassing moments of my life. Ever.

At the *Radar Magazine* event on December 4, 2007.

When I arrived at the event, I was mortified to discover that everybody else was super low-key. Some of the people attending looked like they had just rolled out of bed and hadn't even combed their hair. I was overdressed, and everyone kept looking at me. As you can imagine, I wanted to sink right into the floor. I couldn't wait to get out of that room and take that dress off. If my goal was to stand out from the crowd, I accomplished it, but not in a good way. I don't know what I was thinking—I just saw the word *gala* and figured it meant "formal." Lesson learned: Always, always find out exactly what you've been invited to before you pick up an outfit to wear or trust your point of contact for the event. Or call someone who is already at the event to get the vibe, so you won't have to go through my embarrassment. I sure wish I had. I still shudder when I see pictures of myself in that get-up.

I guess the main moral lesson here is to always remember to be yourself when it comes to events and that everyone doesn't have your best interest in mind. If the outfit doesn't feel right, change it. I think about how far I've come in regards to events and parties and now you can't tell me anything. I know what works for me and that's all that matters.

Funny thing is that shortly after we posted photos from the event, I received an e-mail from a young woman who saw pictures of the dress and said she loved it. She wanted one exactly like it for her prom, and asked me where I bought it. I planned to give it to her, but she never responded to my e-mail. I still have that dress hanging in a closet as my testament to what not being yourself can cost you, not only in cash, but also in swallowed pride.

Now let's talk about what happens when you get invited to cover those events.

Not all sparkle and glamour

A lot of celebrity blog readers think that blogging about celebs translates instantly into parties and red carpets. Like I said before, you have to make a choice as to whether you want to pursue celebrity for yourself or not. If your blog is successful, you're going to attract some personal publicity even if you're not looking for it. I know I have and it brings out the haters. I just don't let them bother me. Some celebrity bloggers (you know who they are) are so egocentric that they start behaving like they're stars too, instead of covering them for their readers. I think it's important to remember that even if you start getting invites to events, you are there to cover the event, not because you yourself are important. If you start forgetting why you're blogging, then you're going to disappoint your readers and lose them.

Concrete Loop is a positive blog. I think there's enough hate in the world as it is and wanted my blog to be a place where readers can go, read about their favorite celebrities, and not feel like we're trashing everybody (I can only do so much about the comment area). As a result of this positive attitude, Concrete Loop gets invited to a lot of events and—very much a plus—we pick up advertising that the negative blogs don't get. Think about it—if you're a major artist and some blogger constantly prints nasty stuff about you, are you really going to want to talk to that blogger at an awards show? Or are you going to buy a bunch of space on that blog when you release your next album? I think the answer is obvious.

That doesn't mean you should kiss butt either. Concrete Loop is honest, but it strives not to be ugly. You can tell the truth without putting all the extras on it.

The celebrity world is full of beautiful people, but believe me when I say they have a lot of help being beautiful. That's not to imply that celebrities aren't extremely attractive people who are also talented and hardworking. They have to address a combination of these things to make it to the top in this really competitive business, but they also work very hard at being beautiful. When you see someone like Rihanna or Janet Jackson looking like a million dollars, what you don't see is the army of people who get her ready for her appearances: Before she steps foot out of the door, hair and makeup people are all over her, not to mention her stylist, dresser, and manicurist. Nothing is left to chance.

And beautiful people like to hang around with beautiful people. Some of the women that big stars have hanging on their arms are amazing looking, and that's not by coincidence. They cultivate other attractive individuals.

When you're covering an event, it's hard not to get sucked into believing that you're there as one of those beautiful people. Maybe you are invited to it, but if you're a celebrity blogger, you are there in your official capacity—not to party and get drunk. And no matter what you think, you're not one of "them." There's a real disconnect on the parts of some bloggers who mistake publicity gestures as friendship. As I said earlier, if you get invited to cover events, they're inviting you to cover events. If that sounds simplistic, it's meant to be. A whole lot of bloggers who get in that position mistake all of that attention for friendship. Although you may form a bond with certain celebs, it's rare that a relationship continues after the blogging is over. At the end of the day it's not about the bloggers at all; it's about their blogs. Celebrities know what the game is. Real recognizes real. If you keep your head on straight, you will too.

Even though I'm sure of my abilities when I'm behind a computer, I used to suffer from severe low self-esteem; but because my parents raised me the right way, I am a strong person. This is important if you blog about celebrities and you're around celebrities, because you're going to find yourself in situations that require a lot of backbone. It's like if you go to a party or an event and find there's lots of cocaine floating around—you need to remember your roots and who you are. No compromises. And no doing something that goes against the way you were brought up in order to fit in.

If you start down that path, then you're going to fail because while it may seem kind of cool when celebs do that stuff, it's not cool at all. I don't mean to judge because it's not my place to do that, but I can tell you that there are a lot of drugs and bad behavior in the entertainment field, and if you're not careful, you can cross a line that shouldn't be crossed. Don't fool yourself into thinking that getting drunk and generally acting a fool makes you cool. It doesn't. And neither does going along with the crowd, especially when it's a high-rolling crowd that is into stuff that would horrify your mama.

I'm not saying that celebrities are all shallow, but in general it doesn't matter what's on the inside where most are concerned. They don't care how good your personality is. These people are into whatever it takes to make it in their careers and they hang around with people who enhance those career choices. They care about superficial stuff, like how people look and their affiliations. Let me tell you a story along those lines.

I'm a full-figured girl and I like myself and who I am. Would I like to drop a couple of pounds? Sure, but I don't let the fact that I'm not a size zero rule my life. My outer self is only one small part of the whole.

Anyway, one of my good friends, Niona Manning, came with me to the Kanye West Glow in the Dark tour back in 2008. I was invited to attend by Kanye and his team, and after the show we proceeded to go backstage. In the backstage area there was this weird security guy that stopped us and asked where we thought we were going. I told him we were meeting Kanye and

PHOTOS: Garry Laws Jr.

Posing backstage with Kanye West during my awkward stage.

his right hand man, Don C., for my blog. He pointed to Niona, who is a very pretty girl, and said, "She can come, but you can't." He actually pointed to me and dissed me straight to my face. He thought we were groupies after the concert trying to get backstage. And yes, there were some groupies backstage after the concert, but we weren't among them. That same fellow didn't know I was the girl from Concrete Loop. A little later, Don C. came up on one of those electronic scooters and said hello and told us to come on and he'd walk us back. You should have seen the look on that security guard's face when we walked past him and were chilling with Kanye backstage.

I have many examples of ways I got dissed by some people in the celebrity world, but I don't let it get to me because at the end of the day I know the game. You have to have thick skin if you want to make moves and get comfortable with being out of your comfort zone.

Motivation and competition

Beyoncé makes it a policy to keep her private life separate from her public life and I do the same. As I said before, when you're working, you're working: Keeping your blogging isolated from your personal life will help you maintain balance.

I started blogging as a personal outlet for myself, and it's proven very satisfying, even if I have been somewhat disillusioned by the worlds celebrities inhabit. If you're fragile and can't take the possibility of finding out that a celebrity you admire is one of the worst people in the world (okay, exaggerating here, but some of them really are not nice people), then celebrity blogging probably is not for you.

I still blog primarily for myself, but I also like getting e-mails from readers who tell me that Concrete Loop helps keep them sane and they enjoy reading the blog between classes or during breaks at work because it helps them relax and clear their minds.

If you want to blog about celebrities, now is a good time because celebrity blogs are really popular. I'm not saying there's a lack of selection—the web is saturated with them, but does this mean you shouldn't launch a celebrity blog of your own? You know the saying "Never say never"? That's what I say too. You can always bring something different to the table, find a way to be unique, and make yourself stand out from the crowd. Many of the celebrity blogs that are popular right now focus on trends. I believe that if you do that, you're also going to die with the trends. Establish your own style and find a different approach—if you really want to blog about celebrities, you can make it work.

Comments

While I've talked about them before, the comments section on a celebrity blog is very different from a comments section on other types of blogs. For one thing—and this is a biggie—on celebrity blogs, people in the industry often read the comments. They check them in order to see what fans like and react to, what catches their attention, and how things are playing: music, videos, movies, even rumors and publicity ventures. Comments are a very important part of a celebrity blog.

Here's something else: People who are connected to celebrities also will read your blog. Concrete Loop used to post a lot of rumors in the early stage, and as you know, I decided to scale back on them. There was just too much drama connected with rumors.

For example, there used to be one person who always commented anytime I ran an item about one particular celebrity. That person would say things like, "Oh yeah, this is true. I know because I used to work for [celebrity's name]." Each time, the celebrity or a person in his team contacted me and tried to get the poster's IP address out of me and made all kinds of threats.

It wasn't worth it to me to keep dealing with it—and no, I didn't give up the information.

I doubt seriously that if you write a food blog, you'll have people bugging you about the identities of your readers, but you'd better believe celebrities are interested in the posts that appear on a celebrity blog! Be prepared to deal with it.

The publicity machine

Another thing that you'll have to deal with as a celebrity blogger is a publicist. In fact, you'll have to deal with lots of them.

Celebrity publicists are a very professional bunch, although to most bloggers they can seem (or be) pushy and annoying. For the most part, though, I have found publicists to be a big help and very thoughtful. Their job is to keep their celebrity client in the public eye and your job is to blog about them—two goals that really work well together.

Publicists and the other people around celebrities are important to you because they can get you up close and personal with that celebrity. Never think the people who work for celebrities don't count—they do. If anything, they are the oil for the machine. From their chefs to their manicurists, these are the individuals the celebrity relies on every day.

Most publicists I work with are cool. I follow them on Twitter and keep up with the activities of the celebrities they are representing. A good relationship with a publicist can really pay off for you, but if you get on their bad side, it can have the opposite effect on your blog and your blogging career. In fact, if you get on the wrong side of anyone in this business, you can find yourself blocked.

For example, I was supposed to appear as a guest on BET's *106 & Park* (a popular video countdown show) in December of 2010. A celebrity was hosting the show and was going to have his favorite bloggers featured, and since he's a fan of Concrete Loop, he invited me. For some reason someone at BET doesn't like Concrete Loop or me—I don't know who or why, but whoever it is pretty much blocks me anytime there is a BET event. There is always some type of random hassle my contributors and I have to go through to get basic clearance at their events. Long story short, I never got on the show, and at the end of the day it was their loss.

That just goes to show that if you're on the bad side of someone in the celebrity world, there are certain places you can't go, but it doesn't mean you won't be successful. Whoever blocked me at BET may control the road to *106 & Park* but they don't control the road to my success. The whole experience has left a bad taste in my mouth, but it's typical of the way some people operate. I always say, karma does not play, so they will get theirs.

Angel's Bonus:
Let's Party!

We all love a good party, and we all love to read about celebs and the events they attend. The photos are fun and who doesn't like analyzing their style? After all, there's nothing more interesting than a celeb misstep when dressing for a big event. And yeah, there's that catty little thrill that comes from seeing a big star show up on the red carpet looking like he or she lost a fight with a coyote. Not that we're drawn to failure—it's just that there is something about a person with access to designer clothes, a stylist, top-notch hair and makeup artists, dressers, manicurists, and a whole army of others who *still* gets it wrong that makes us curious. You know what? Sometimes that big fashion faux pas on the red carpet *isn't* a mistake, but a calculated way to get publicity. You know the old saying about how "it doesn't matter what they're saying about me, as long as they're talking"? Well, that explains how a lot of celebrities end up hitting step and repeat looking like they bought their outfits at the Goodwill.

Step and repeat. That's what they call the place where the celebs stop and pose for the cameras on the red carpet. I thought it was the most glamorous place possible until my job took me to so many of those moments. For celebrities, posing over and over and over for the paparazzi to get their pictures all over the wires, in the magazines, and even on shows like *Fashion Police* is simply part of the job. In fact, with celebs, even attending parties is mostly work. Glamorous work, but work nonetheless.

I've been invited to my share of parties since I founded Concrete Loop, but they're not all as exciting as they may seem when you're a blogger. I'm not there to let my hair down and have a good time, but to report on what's happening, get pictures, and bring them back so readers can see how the other half lives. And recently, I even threw a party of my own, or Concrete Loop did, and hundreds of lucky fans got to attend that bash. If you didn't, this is the chapter where I'll take you behind all of the action and show you how much work is involved in getting things done the right way.

But first, let's head for California and visit a party thrown by Kanye West. And no, it wasn't a typical celebrity party. But, hey, it's Kanye West—that should explain everything.

Kanye's West Coast get-together

Kanye's party for *808s & Heartbreak* was probably one of the most interesting and strangest parties I've ever attended. I received the invitation from him and wasn't going to attend since it was in California and I was still in North Carolina at the time. But the invite wouldn't leave my mind and finally I thought, "I've got to go to this one. If I don't, then I'm stupid." So I flew alone to attend the album release party.

When I arrived at the event, I was relieved to find I was on the list and the guy checking it even knew who I was. Believe me, making sure your name is "on the list" is a hassle, and as I flew all the way from the East Coast for the event, a mistake like that would have been a mess.

Kanye held the event at this empty warehouse. Guests had to walk up this ramp into this waiting room. We were all waiting for the go-ahead to go into the main room and I was looking around when I noticed that I was standing next to will.i.am of the Black Eyed Peas. We had a little small talk—the back-and-forth kind of chatter you have with anyone who is standing next to you in line. I just thought it was funny, how I was in the VIP line with celebs.

There were tons of people there. When I got the invitation, I thought it was going to be a medium-sized event, kind of like many of the other album releases I attended. I don't know what I was thinking—this was Kanye West. He doesn't do anything in a medium-sized way.

I saw a couple of other bloggers across the way and we were all waiting around when they told us we could proceed into the next room. We walked into this room that had all kinds of odd lighting and naked ladies standing in the middle of it. And I do mean fully naked, as in the-day-they-were-born naked. And this guy starts yelling, "No cameras! I mean it. No cameras! I don't care who you are—I don't care if you're Jay-Z or Beyoncé! I'd better not see any cameras! If you pull out a camera, you'll get kicked out of here!"

At this point we're all thinking, "Ooooookay..." All the dudes there were loving it because the girls were not only naked, but very pretty, but another girl says to me, "I thought this was a listening party," and I said, "Me too." Then we see Kanye coming in and he waits until everyone gets in before he starts talking. Kanye then says that all of this represents what he feels the visuals of the album are. He wanted to have a listening party like no one else had ever had before.

Then the lights started dimming and the room was turning into this blue landscape. One of the security guards there—he was acting like he was crazy—started cussing at Mos Def because he was taking pictures on his cell phone. The guard was yelling at Mos Def, "Put that phone down! I don't care who you are!"

Kanye was making his rounds, the lights were dimming and changing colors, and the (naked) girls were standing there, but then they started to change their positions, and then changed them again. It was just very weird. It was dark and I really couldn't see who was in the room, but all of a sudden it hit me and I thought "Oh my God, I am standing next to Rick Ross! Oh my God, that's Mos Def! Oh my God, that's Jay-Z! Oh my God, that's Tracee Ellis Ross [Diana Ross's daughter] from *Girlfriends*!" I just kept looking around and not knowing what to think. And the lights kept going on and off, on and off.

I was standing there next to popular rapper Rick Ross and Rick was dancing and going all crazy and having a good time. Then Kanye stood next to me and I tapped him on he shoulder and he said, "Oh, Angel. Thank you for coming," and he gave me a hug. Then he took me over to their little VIP area, the roped-off area with the security guards, and he introduced me to Jay-Z. Jay-Z was nonchalant in shades (despite it being so dark) and had a couple of security guards next to him, both with guns.

Kanye said, "This is Angel from Concrete Loop." Kanye was kind of tipsy—I don't think he really knew what was going on at that point.

Jay-Z was sitting there chilling and said, "Oh, everyone reads Concrete Loop." At that point I felt like I was in the twilight zone. I thanked him. Kanye disappeared after that—I think he left and I slowly made my way out of VIP.

I didn't have a car since I had taken a cab there and Cali isn't like New York City, where cabs are everywhere. I had to walk across the street, call a cab to come get me, and then wait for it to arrive to take me back to the hotel. It was a headache, but in the end well worth it. Even though I didn't have any real photos (just one on my iPhone) I was happy I went.

An iPhone photo I took of the girls standing in the middle of the room at Kanye's party.

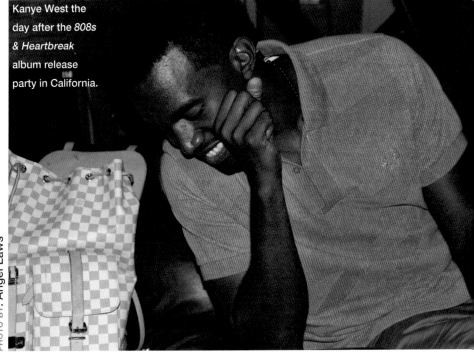

Kanye West the day after the *808s & Heartbreak* album release party in California.

PHOTO BY: Angel Laws

The next day, I e-mailed one of Kanye's assistants and asked him if I could have some pictures for a blog post I was working on. Kanye only had one photographer there so I wanted to cover my bases. They said they couldn't give me pics, but they could invite me to the studio with Kanye. Of course I went and in the end I landed some exclusive content for Concrete Loop. At the studio session, Kanye said in reference to the party the night before, "No one can ever say they've thrown a party like that. VIPs mixing with industry people, mixing with bloggers, mixing with regular people. It was dope!"

It was dope—and to think that originally I wasn't even going to go!

Where were you when the girl's hair caught on fire?

And then there was Diddy's infamous penthouse party where the girl's hair caught on fire. I was there when it happened, but not on the floor where the girl lit up. Literally. Here's the story:

Diddy held his party in New York at the London Hotel, a nice Manhattan-based hotel. It was in the penthouse, the hotel's top two floors. The elevator takes penthouse guests up to the top floor, where the entertainment and living areas of the penthouse are located. There are magnificent views on three sides, with windows looking out over Central Park, the Manhattan skyline, and the Hudson River.

The entire suite has 2,500 square feet. On the bottom floor is a table that seats about eight people, a kitchen (the chef at the London is Gordon Ramsay from *Hell's Kitchen* fame), and a huge living area with this enormous fourteen-foot curved sofa that dominates the room. The place is decorated mostly in neutrals—grays and tans—with some blues.

There's a staircase that connects the fifty-fourth floor and that leads up to two bedrooms with king-size beds and huge marble bathrooms. Anyone who saw the girl in the tub with her hair on fire will recognize one of the marble soaking tubs on the second floor of the penthouse.

I don't know how much it costs to rent the penthouse for a couple of days, but I do know the hotel charges an extra $3,000 to stage an event there (and that's in addition to the room rental fee). Money like that pays my bills, but for a celebrity like Diddy, it's a drop in the bucket.

When Taj Washington (noted celebrity photographer), Daniel Dejene (celebrity event planner/PR specialist), and I arrived at the party, there was this long, long line in the lobby. We went up to the lady who was checking people in to see what the deal was. She said, "You can't go up because we're over capacity. You may need to come back later."

I was like, "What?"

She explained that because it was a hotel, the lobby could only hold so many people. I assume it had something to do with the fire code. I guess someone came up and told her I was from Concrete Loop or something because we were two seconds from leaving when she said, "Oh, Angel from Concrete Loop?" And I told her that was correct, and she said, "Oh, you definitely can come up, but we're over capacity." She told us the hotel had a restaurant and we could wait there, and that Diddy said everything was on him.

We went into the restaurant and had a couple of drinks while we waited; I thought it was really cool of them to comp them. We didn't order any food, but we could have— in fact, Taj was close to getting something to eat when, after about thirty minutes, the woman told us we could go up.

We went to the elevator and were passing this long line of people—and there were some celebrities too, like Fabolous and Trey Songz, and people were saying, "Who is that? Why does she get to go in?" You could feel the heat in the air. I had the feeling it was going to be a weird night (and I was right).

As soon as I stepped off the elevator—carefully, as Diddy was streaming the party live on UStream and had all of these production people and equipment everywhere—and entered the penthouse, I started seeing celebrities, like Dawn and Kalenna from Dirty Money. There's a DJ and girls everywhere. There were girls going upstairs and girls coming downstairs and

PHOTO: Taj Washington

Chilling with Laurieann at the Diddy party.

celebrities kissing on girls. People on that big, expensive curved couch—drunk. It was kind of overwhelming. I was there for about an hour without talking to Diddy (and Diddy was all over the place), then that hour turned into another hour. Since he invited me, I was like okay can I get my exclusive now?

Here's the truth about celebrity parties: They're not like our parties. When I go to a party, I socialize and kick back, but celebrity parties aren't like that at all. The celebrity host isn't worried about you or whether you're enjoying the party at all. Unless he sees you, you're not even going to cross his mind, and I'm not the kind of person who is thirsty for attention.

People were coming up and talking to me, like Quincy, Diddy's son. He was really sweet and introduced himself, as if I didn't know who he was. Another person I met was popular choreographer Laurieann Gibson.

Lauriann Gibson has had an amazing career. She choreographed many of Lady Gaga's numbers, from "Poker Face" to "Telephone," and has choreographed everyone from Keri Hilson to Alicia Keys to Nicki Minaj.

We had actually put a post up that day about her and she came up to me and said she really appreciated the post and thanked Concrete Loop for always showing her so much love.

The party was still going strong, but I was ready to go home. Too many people, too much smoke, lots of noise—my own bed was sounding really good to me. I told Taj that I was going to head home and he decided to stay so he could get more photos. I still hadn't talked to Diddy, but it was time for me to go.

I was heading out and saw three security guards by the door. I saw Daniel and I also told him I was leaving and then discovered I had just missed the elevator, so I stood there and waited for it to come back up. The wait took forever—it takes a long time for an elevator to get to the penthouse level. I started having a conversation with this one security guard, the usual "have a good night" stuff, when the elevator finally arrived. I stepped in and the doors were literally closing when Diddy came out of the side door and jumped into the elevator. The door opened back up and Diddy said, "Where do you think you're going?"

I told him, "I'm going home." Then he gave me a hug and said, "You're not going anywhere. I haven't shown Concrete Loop any love yet." The timing was actually perfect. Although I was tired and set on going home, for some strange reason I was amped again.

We walked back into the party and singer/model Cassie came out of the other elevator. Diddy asked if we knew each other and she said, yes, that we had met at Fashion Week. Cassie is a good friend of Concrete Loop music contributor Brian Davis.

Diddy told the security

Diddy and I behind the DJ booth at the party.

PHOTO: Taj Washington

guard that he was to stay with me for the rest of the night and told him to give me anything I wanted. Then he said he had to go organize some things and when he came back, we'd go behind the DJ's booth and talk. I waited on the side and talked to the security guard. I said I need to get my photographer if we're going behind the DJ's booth, so we went looking for Taj among the party guests. The security guard was pushing people out of the way and clearing a path for me. We finally located Taj, who was wondering what the heck was going on—suddenly we were all official.

Diddy came back in with Cassie and everyone was making way for them and telling Cassie how beautiful she is. We went behind the DJ booth and that's where we filmed the video that we had on Concrete Loop showing Diddy giving us a shout-out and saying how much he loves the site. I got a gift bag that had a Flip video camera in it, some DiddyBeats earphones, coupons, Sean John shirts, all types of stuff was in that bag. I thought it was really dope that he showed us how much he liked Concrete Loop. Most of the items later came in handy for an exclusive giveaway on the site.

Funny thing is that while this was happening, I was getting all these texts and e-mails and tweets from people who were watching the UStream of the party asking if that was really me, because they had just seen me on the video with Diddy. That was crazy. It was also one of the most interesting party experiences I have ever had.

Concrete Loop throws a party of its own

Parties are a big part of the celebrity world. It's something I didn't really think too much about until I started blogging and getting invited to all of these parties and events. I found out that it's way harder to throw a good party than it looks. It's not just a matter of picking up some wine and inviting your friends to stop by. The celebrities who go to those events all look so dope, and there are all these cool gift bags that get handed out. It seems very glamorous and exciting and some of it is—but it's also a lot of work and nothing like what you think it's going to be like.

In November of 2010 Concrete Loop turned five. Brian Davis, who is the music contributor to the site (I've mentioned Brian before), had always wanted the site to throw an event. When Kanye first shouted us out on his song, Brian was saying we needed to host an event. Frankly, I was scared no one would show up and I also thought the timing wasn't right yet. I had been to a few blogger events (no, I'm not going to name names) and there were only a few people there. When you go to all of the trouble and expense of throwing a party and only ten people bother to come, it's not only embarrassing, but a waste of time and money.

When no one comes or the party flops, it's a reflection of your brand as well as you as a blogger, so no one (except maybe some of the snarkier competition) wants to see your party turn out bad. When Brian kept pushing me to hold an event for Concrete Loop, all I could think of was that this could be a real disaster if we weren't careful.

Then the perfect opportunity arose. Not only was it Concrete Loop's birthday, but we were also relaunching the website. That gave me two projects to work on: a party and the relaunch.

I had never thrown a really big event like that, nor did I really know what I was getting myself into, so I made the smartest decision ever and hired an event planner. Not just any event planner either but the terrific Daniel Dejene.

Daniel is a professional's professional. He sweats all the small stuff so the person throwing the party can worry about other things, like whether the guests will get along, will the celebrities invited actually show up, and are there enough gift bags to go around—the things you don't want to deal with when you're the host and already have a million balls in the air.

I met Daniel through singer/songwriter Estelle. The funny thing is I met him even before I moved to New York and he told me if I ever moved to the Big Apple and needed an event planner, he was my man, and I thought at the time, "Yeah, right. If I ever move to New York." Little did I know...

Daniel is probably best known for planning events for Academy Award–winning actor Forest Whitaker and his actress-wife, Keisha, so I was in good hands. In the celebrity world, no one does this alone. It's not a birthday party, backyard production kind of thing. You have to have someone who knows what he's doing.

Daniel asked me for my vision of the party and my guest list. As a celebrity blogger, I knew I would be expected to have some type of celebrity performance, so I started calling all of these celebs I'd helped out in the past when no one knew who they were. I won't drop names, but there was one actor/rapper in particular that I thought would be easy to get to make an appearance. Concrete Loop was not only the first major blog to post anything about his mixtapes, but we were also the first blog to say he had star potential in the rap world before he got his major deal. I used to talk to him and text with him all the time, and in the beginning he was down with doing it, but when

Chilling with Keri Hilson backstage at the Essence Music Festival.

PHOTO BY: Taj Washington

the time came, he wouldn't even return my phone calls. I was referred to "his people." In the celebrity world they have a whole bunch of assistants and PR people. And they were telling me, "Oh, he gets paid for performing." Of course I knew that, but after all the promotion and love I'd given him, you would think I would have got the discount price. I was quoted some pretty outrageous prices, like as much as $75,000 for a performance or appearance. That was way out of our overall budget, even with Kodak as a sponsor.

I called another performer, actually the first person interviewed on Concrete Loop, and she's a nice person and all, but the price I was quoted was ridiculous. I was actually very naive about getting celebrities to help out at the party. I had a budget, and even though Concrete Loop is successful, I don't make anywhere near what these celebrities pull down.

A few people did come through for me, keeping their word. I definitely want to give props to singer/songwriter Keri Hilson. I'll never say anything negative about her after the love she showed us. A lot of people hate on her in the blog world, but at the end of the day she keeps her word. I saw her in New Orleans at the *Essence* Music Festival and asked if she would make an appearance at a party we planned on throwing later that year. She said she'd definitely be there and just to keep her in the loop. When it was time to come, she did and she even performed. I didn't have to pay her anything and she even stuck around to speak to her fans. I thought that was dope. Those experiences opened my eyes on the business end as to how celebrities can and do behave sometimes. Despite acting like it sometimes, not everyone is your friend and most celebrities will only contact you when they need something. Lesson learned.

Back to the party, Keri and soul singer Goapele both performed at the event. Goapele set the whole vibe of the party with her song "Closer." It was amazing to see someone I idolized when I was a teen dedicating a song to me, especially a song that helped me through some bad times. It was like everything had come full circle.

There's more to organizing a party than a guest list

Planning a guest list and getting celebs to show was just one part of organizing the party. I also had to find a venue. Things in New York are expensive—not as expensive as Los Angeles is, but it's not like renting out the pizza spot in the middle of nowhere either.

We looked at a lot of places, some of them fairly small. We couldn't throw much of a party in a place with room for only 150 people, and the prices were crazy—like $30,000. Then Daniel found the Hiro Ballroom, and they had a great package with a stage and a VIP area for the celebrities. And I wanted to make sure there was adequate space for the party's guests of honor—Concrete Loop's readers. The whole point of the relaunch was to make it something our readers would enjoy.

Luckily I was working with Aisling Mcdonagh and Judith Heimowitz at Buzz Media because we were able to attract some big sponsors, like Kodak. Kodak sponsored a photo booth with the Kodak logo and people could take free pictures that were then displayed on the wall. And since it was an evening event, we also secured a liquor sponsor, Belvedere Vodka.

I had to pay out of pocket for Concrete Loop merchandise for the gift bags and that involved its own set of drama. The day before the event we got word from the people who were printing the T-shirts that they might not be done in time for the event. Here's a tip I learned from Daniel: When you're ordering something like this, always say you need it a day earlier than you really do. It gives you a little bit of a safety zone. Fortunately for us, it all worked out, but it was nerve-wracking trying to get it all sorted out.

Then we had a problem with the logos. Kodak didn't like the way their logo looked on some poster placements, and since some of their people were based out of Los Angeles, the posters had to be edited and shipped from there.

My vision for the Concrete Loop party was that it had to have a nice vibe and be laid-back. I didn't want anyone to be overdressed (you know I know what I'm talking about) and to come wearing their own style. The Hiro Ballroom could hold about seven hundred to eight hundred people and at one point we were over capacity, so they locked the door. Some celebrities couldn't get in and my friend, Huny, a graphic designer and blogger, was having issues with the security guard at the door. It got a little heated, but eventually they let her in.

Most everybody there was a Concrete Loop fan and one fan, Maya AnToinique, won the Kodak-sponsored contest. She was flown to the event, got a car service, and Kodak gave her a camera to take pictures. It was nice and I think she enjoyed it.

One thing that took getting used to was being on the "step and repeat" myself. As soon as I got there, the cameras were flashing and I had reporters from *The New York Times*, *USA Today*, and lots of other places trying to interview me. I had to do some thinking on my feet because as you know, I'm used to doing the asking, not the answering. I was also grateful that most of the photos turned out okay.

Throwing together an event also taught me why celebrities hire assistants. A lot of people were shoving their business cards at me and telling me they were photographers or makeup artists and lots of other things. If I would have had a personal assistant, I could have mingled a little more at the party because you can have your assistant aid you by getting the cards and

PHOTO BY: Rafael Fondeur

A photo of me speaking to the crowd during the event.

information while you chill a bit. I waded through a lot of people that night. Some people who were in there were just trying to get a job and I can't blame them because it was New York City, city of the hustler.

The party was well publicized and well attended. In addition to Keri Hilson and Goapele, Sway from MTV, rapper Jim Jones, Terence J from BET, and Omarion also showed up. Estelle was in the studio recording or she would have been there too. Kanye and Diddy both tweeted about the party. They said they were sorry to miss it, but honestly, this was a party for the readers of Concrete Loop. Those were the real VIPs.

Overall I enjoyed the event and Daniel and his team did a great job. But as always I had to get back home and go to work on the coding and postings for the site because we were relaunching the next day. Plus, I needed to round up the photos, get stuff together for Kodak to show them what we did, reply to a billion e-mails, and blog about the event.

Dope party? Most definitely, but I didn't get any sleep for days.

Angel's Bonus Photos

Check out a few photos of me with some of the celebrities I have met over the past few years.

Angel with producer/enter-tainer Pharrell Williams and producer Shay after she interviewed them in California.

PHOTOGRAPHER: Taj Washington

PHOTOGRAPHER: Taj Washington

Angel pictured with singer/songwriter Bilal.

PHOTOGRAPHER: Taj Washington

Angel speaks on stage at the Fifth Anniversary Concrete Loop Party in New York City.

Angel pictured with singers Dawn (L) and Kalenna (R) of Dirty Money at their album release party in New York City.

PHOTOGRAPHER: Taj Washington

Angel pictured backstage in New Orleans with singer Estelle.

PHOTOGRAPHER: Taj Washington

Singer Solange
Knowles and Angel
backstage in Chicago
after Solange's
performance.

Angel pictured with singer/musician/producer Wyclef Jean after interviewing him at the Buzz Media office in New York City.

Angel Wraps It All Up

Concrete Loop started as a hobby. While making money was always one of my ambitions, I never dreamed something I enjoyed doing in my free time could also turn into a profession. In this chapter, I'm going to review some of the things we've talked about in this book, look back over that journey from college student to entrepreneur, and touch on some new concepts, like how to build yourself a team. We'll start with the recap.

Concrete Loop grew out of my personal frustration at being unable to find stories and pictures of the black celebrities I found interesting. I built a blog to fulfill a personal need and inadvertently tapped into a universal demand for the same thing.

Lots of successful entrepreneurs come into their own when they find solutions to problems they have experienced themselves. Since the Internet, many online businesses have been jump-started by individuals just like you who saw a demand and created a solution. In fact, countless African American–owned businesses got their start by recognizing the needs of an underserved community.

The thing is, the ground floor still has plenty of room for those of us with good ideas. It may sometimes seem like all of the good ones have already been taken (like the joke about where all the good men are), but that's not really the case. Concrete Loop is a solid example of how you can find a profitable, workable idea in your everyday life and make it pay. Just like writers are told to write about what they know, you should tap into your own knowledge bank to find the next big thing. Find your inspiration and work it. I managed to turn frustration into a solution, maybe you will do the same. Or, maybe you'll find yours in your hobbies, your job, or even something you've dreamed about, but the main thing is to make the commitment to do whatever it takes to turn your idea into a blog and then turn that into the success you envision. No genie is going to hop out of a bottle and no magic wand is going to wave. How much you achieve will depend entirely on the decisions you make and how hard you work; the bad news is you're going to have to work really hard because there's a lot of competition out there. The good news is that the tools you need to turn your blog into a moneymaker are at your disposal. You simply have to access them.

So, get your resolve on and roll up your sleeves. Whether your blog turns into a big moneymaker or not, you will find value in starting it. Keep in mind that everything about your blogging business will be subject to trial and error. The first idea you have may not be the one you end up taking to the finish line. If you have setbacks or second thoughts about the direction in which you're going, that's fine. It's your blog and you can change your mind, direction, or focus whenever you want. I make changes to Concrete Loop all the time, and you can do the same. So, let's review some of the steps we've covered in this book and talk a little girl talk while we're doing it.

Don't be discouraged by the numbers

When I say millions of people are blogging, I mean that millions start blogs. Not everyone who starts a blog actually continues to keep it going.

Blogging isn't easy (that should be evident by the amount of blogs that are abandoned). As a profession, it requires time, commitment, and the capacity to learn new things. Many start because they want to have an online presence, then they find that updating a blog is work. If your blog isn't your day job, finding time to keep it competitive can be daunting; but if you want it to succeed, you're going to have to turn off your favorite show, pass on that chance to have drinks with the girls, or even get up a little earlier every morning so you can update and work online before you head for your paying job.

That's not what you want to hear, but it's true. Unless you stumble across a fabulous idea or have access to people and information that will make your blog stand out from the beginning, you will have to dedicate a lot of time and effort into building it. Heck, even if you attract a lot of attention, you still have to amass a respectable traffic pattern to get advertisers interested. When it comes to blogs, there really is no such thing as an overnight success or a shortcut.

So, even though millions of people start blogs and there are millions of blogs out there, the ones that go the distance are much fewer in number. Add to that the blogs that are never going to be your competition—different interests, noncommercial, or something that's only for someone's family—and you narrow down that scary-sounding number even more.

Still, it's good to look at the stats when you're trying to decide on a topic and an angle. After all, not everyone has the desire to blog for commercial success—you do, and that sets you apart from the pack.

Narrowing that topic

Finding and angling the right topic is more important than having a track record when it comes to the Internet. You can always learn HTML, but you can't substitute picking the right place from which to push off your new blog. This is where you want to brainstorm.

I don't advocate the simple route here, and by that I mean picking a broad topic and jumping in. There are exceptions to this, though. If you have a unique "in" on the subject—if your BFF is a fashion designer or pro golfer—then, yeah, talk about fashion in general or pro golfing because you have an insider who can steer you to stories. Or if your own career takes you places that few others can go, then by all means jump on it. But, if you're like most of us, this doesn't apply.

For regular people like us, there has to be something special about our blogs to get them noticed. I chose black celebrities and concentrated on stars and up-and-coming performers who weren't getting the attention of the mainstream press. That set Concrete Loop apart from other blogs out there because most were covering the Will Smith, Denzel Washington, Hallie Berry news and hardly anyone but the fans were paying attention to the performers who weren't household names.

This is something you need to remember when you're choosing what to write about. You need to focus on something narrow enough to be niche, but not so narrow that there's nowhere to go with it. For example, if you have a site dedicated to one particular performer, unless you have a personal or business relationship with that performer, you're going to run out of material pretty fast. And face it, even if you eat, drink, and breathe news about Missy Elliott, what do you do with your blog when nothing is going on? Sure, you'll get random hits, but your traffic will dip unless you can keep updating with new stuff. And can you sell enough advertising to make money off your blog? You might sell some advertising, but not a lot. Advertisers want to reach as many people as possible when they buy ad space. So maybe instead of focusing on Missy alone, why not look at black female performers? You can even narrow that down a bit by type of music, era, etc. The trick is to pick a subject, narrow it, angle it, and still have enough material to make daily blogging feasible.

I suggested earlier that you make a list of subjects you might want to blog about and combine them to come up with something unique. Try that exercise, and if nothing jumps out at you, expand the list and make copies. Then sit down with the copies and randomly draw lines back and forth to see what combinations you come up with. You might be surprised at the possibilities.

And keep in mind that there really are some places you don't want to go. Porn really is not a good idea, and neither is anything that smacks of racism or extremism. No matter what your interests are, you can't ever lose sight of the fact that the people you ultimately have to please in order to make money are the advertisers. They aren't going to buy space on a porn blog or one that pushes hate.

Naming your baby

Although you can change your blog's name if you decide it doesn't work, it's a whole lot better to start off with a winner the first go around. Unlike some performers who change their name (or its spelling) at the drop of a hat, you can't keep changing the name of your blog without your readers getting confused and possibly compromising the blog's branding.

And that's another good point: You are going to expend a lot of effort and spend a lot of money (at least proportionately) to start your brand. You need a clear idea of who and what you are and how that ties in with your name before you commit a lot of your time and money into promoting it.

Consider, for example, how some female celebrities take their husband's last name and add it to theirs when they marry. Sometimes the marriage works and sometimes it doesn't. When it doesn't, the celeb usually ends up having to change her name back and drop the spouse. That's confusing for some fans. Your blog name should reflect your uniqueness but never be confusing. One way to ensure that is to go with some version of your own name. The problem with this is that using your name will tie you irrevocably to your blog. Even if you sell it or take on a partner, you won't be able to separate yourself from the blog if you brand it properly.

Of course, if you're interested in pursuing celebrity for yourself, naming your blog after yourself could help. Sure, sure, everyone wants to be a celebrity, but it's not always a good thing to be tied to your blog. I recommend breaking your personal and blog identities into distinct camps so that you can capitalize on both your business and personal pursuits without having one take over the other.

I could give up my ties to Concrete Loop much easier from a corporate standpoint than I could cut ties to my other blog, Angelonfire. If I sold Concrete Loop, I could walk away with no obligations to it, but I couldn't do that with Angelonfire because I *am* Angel. I can't turn that part of me off.

And like I said earlier in the book, buying your name domain is always a good idea, even if you only park it and leave it there. It costs very little to keep a domain and owning your domain could come in handy up the road if you need it. (Check around the net for coupons and you could get a domain for a year for a couple of bucks. And don't ask how many I own. Some women have fewer pairs of shoes!) Buying your name domain keeps at bay the potential embarrassment of having something totally inappropriate associated with your name. If your name's not available, try a variation of it, and keep looking back. Lots of people lose interest in a domain or just plain forget to renew and you can snatch it right up.

When you're fishing around for that perfect blog name, think of all of the people you know who hate the names their mommas gave them. You know, the guy in your class whose mom thought it was a great idea to name the kid after his great-uncle Dudley (not that Dudley isn't a perfectly fine name). He may grow into liking Dudley, but until he does, he'll probably want his friends to call him by a nickname. The lesson here is to name your child (blog) something that will go the distance.

Another point I want to recap here: Pick a name people can remember. If you go for something that's so clever that nobody can remember what it is, then, guess what? Nobody is going to remember it (duh) and you're going to be like the girl no one asked out—sitting all by yourself with a pint of ice cream and a bunch of chick flicks on Saturday night. Only instead of not going out, you're not going to be making any money off your blog, no matter how hard you work at it.

Don't forget, the name's the first thing you learn about a person, and it's also the first thing you learn about a blog. Think of it this way, if your BFF says to you, "I want to set you up with a guy I know. His name's Ty [or Kris or Donnell]." What do you picture? Okay, now she says the same thing, only this guy's name is Hambone (or Beezus or Mergatroyd). Yeah, no matter how hot old Hambone might be, it's kind of tough to picture a guy who calls himself Hambone as sexy. So, fair or not, remember that the name is out there first, and if you choose something that's not in keeping with what your blog is like, you'll spend a lot of time living it down. And probably wishing you had chosen better the first time around.

All that SEO stuff

Depending on how you look at it, search engine optimization is either dead or really important. I'm in the camp that thinks SEO is important. I think it's vital to realize what words will make your website pop up higher in searches. For that you need to do a little research.

It's important not to underrate your search engine results. A high ranking on a big search engine (and they don't come any bigger than Google, although Bing is picking up steam) can translate into huge returns for you, not just in readership, but also in advertising dollars. Advertisers follow traffic, and when traffic beats a path to your door, CoverGirl and L'Oreal won't be too far behind.

To be a success when it comes to SEO keywords, you need to find the words that will work for your blog, and that's completely subject dependent. In other words, it's like finding the right accessories for the outfit you plan to wear on your date.

Think of your blog as your little black dress. Now you're going to accessorize it based on where you and your date are going. If it's casual, let's say a party at some friend's house with a jug of wine, then you'll probably slip into some flats and a cardigan. If your date's taking you to a Broadway show with dinner at a pricey French restaurant, then you'll climb into your tallest, sexiest heels and add a little bling to the mix. Think of keywords as flats and heels.

You'll use different keywords depending on the target audience for your blog and the subject you cover. A shopping blog will cover different territory than a blog dedicated to celebrities or raising kids. But you have to remember to refine your keywords even more than that: A shopping blog that focuses on thrift shops will have some differentiation in keywords than one that targets designer samples.

The best go-to tool for SEO is the Google AdWords Keyword Tool. Check out the keywords that best fit your blog and remember that keywords can be embedded in many different places, including in your site's navigation, page description, the text stand-in for images, and your meta and anchor tags.

Becoming a brand

It's not easy thinking of yourself or your work as a brand, but if you're going to succeed, you need to challenge that thinking. Part of blogging success is offering your readers what they want while putting your own distinct twist on it. Branding is not only a way to offer readers (and advertisers) something unique to your blog, but also the ticket to bigger bucks—and fame, if that's your game.

The important consideration when it comes to branding is you must remember to carry it forward into everything that has anything to do with your blog. Remember what I said about consistency? It's especially valid when it comes to establishing a brand.

Part of becoming a brand is to develop a look that is unique. Using skins, theme colors, logos, even a catch phrase can help set your blog apart from the pack. Think about how when you see certain logos, you immediately associate the product or the company with it. That's what you're striving for—something that will give you immediate identification.

And be original when you develop a logo. People will notice when you copy others. For example, the ad world buzzed when the Rio Olympics Committee unveiled its new logo and someone pointed out how much it looks like the logo of a nonprofit out of Colorado. There's a good chance it was all a coincidence. Two people can have the same idea or ideas that are very similar, but you want to avoid intentional copying.

When you find the perfect logo, consider using it on merchandise and giveaways. You can have calendars, cups, hats, and tote bags printed pretty cheaply these days and they make perfect giveaways. If you don't have the resources to do that yet, buy inexpensive giveaways like iTune downloads. For $5, you have a prize someone will win and have cultivated a lifelong reader of your blog at the same time.

Also, depending on how you market your blog, you may one day want to sell branded merchandise. If you look at the mechanics of branding as something that may one day make you a few bucks, you will see a different aesthetic. In the meantime, before you sell your first T-shirt, put your logo on one and wear it. Make bumper stickers and novelty hats with your blog's logo on them. Share them with people and get your name out there. Those are cheap, easy ways to get publicity and stir up interest everywhere you go.

Diving off your platform into a pool of money

Platform has probably become the most overworked word in the English language, at least as far as the media is concerned, but you can't discount its importance to the success of your blog.

Platform has several meanings, but in blogging it's all about what program you use to blog. Like I said earlier, there are lots of them out there, but for me, WordPress is king. I like the simplicity, adaptability, and searchability of WordPress.

I will admit to a bias: WordPress has brought me nothing but success. It has many pluses to recommend it, but the fact that it allows you to learn as you go along is probably the most important feature for a new blogger. If you have limited experience on the Internet, then you're going to have a steeper learning curve. A platform that allows you to learn as you go along can get you up and running faster, which in turn means you'll build up a readership and be ready to sell advertising quicker than with a platform that isn't so forgiving.

No matter what platform you choose—and there are a lot of them out there—just be sure that you're using something that *you* like. You're the only one who has to be pleased with its performance.

Don't forget your manners

Blogging is still evolving as an art form, so the rules are either nonexistent or flexible, but there *are* generally accepted rules that govern blogging and bloggers in general. Let's take a quick look at what's generally accepted as the two most important rules of blogging netiquette:

1. Don't "borrow" content from other bloggers without permission or proper attribution. Yes, I do sound like a broken record on this one, but if other bloggers find out you're ripping them off, your reputation as a blogger will be scorched and the community will turn on you. If you want to use something another blogger has written, then post a snippet (that means a tiny bit, not half a page) and link to the other blog. That way you'll send traffic to the other blogger (a good thing and you might get some reciprocation) and you'll also stay out of hot water, both legally and ethically.

2. Keep your paws off of other bloggers' photos, logos, and art. If you don't have permission to use it, then it's not yours to use. Like a blog post or other written content, you can link to photos, but you can't lift them. And it's never, ever acceptable to copy someone's style. You can be inspired by another site, but don't ride on their coattails. Create your own unique one instead.

Remember that there are thousands and thousands of people on the net and eventually a reader is going to spot it if you're lifting material from someone else. In fact, this is a good place to stop and recap the plagiarism issue.

The Internet is crowded with people who want to be writers, bloggers, graphic artists, photographers, etc. And there are some very talented people out there who succeed in doing just that, but there are also a lot of pretenders. Those pretenders think they can take someone else's material and put it under their own names and pass it off as their own work. Sometimes they get away with it—for a while. Eventually, though, the real owner of the work always finds out. Here's how I feel about people who rip off the hard work of others: They're nothing but thieves. Period. My intellectual property is mine and mine alone, and if I give someone permission to reprint it, then that's fine, but pretending you wrote it (or reprinting it in full without permission, even if you credit me) is not only dishonest, it's a violation of copyright. So don't do it.

Check and see if anyone is using your work without your permission. One way to see if your stuff is being mentioned (or reprinted without your permission) is to do a vanity search on a large search engine like Google and see what turns up. You might be surprised (and dismayed) at where you find your stuff.

Know who is singing in your choir

You know that expression "You're preaching to the choir"? Well, your choir is your readership. They love what you love and that's why they're reading it. And when I say, "Know your readers," I'm not talking about knowing them personally (although you do want a certain amount of hands on interplay with them), I am referring to knowing who they are in terms of demographics, what they like (or don't like) about your site, and what their expectations are.

And that means you need to be somewhat predictable. I am not saying you should be boring. Boring should never be an option for your blog. You can always introduce new features into the mix, but you shouldn't stray so far from what your readers have grown to know and love about your blog that they don't recognize it. In other words, don't tinker with the core of your success. Your readers need to know that the basics aren't going to change— that you will still be covering the things they come to you for, but that doesn't mean you can't add some new features and change things up a little from time to time.

If you get anything out of this book (and I hope you get a lot of good tips, a template for putting together a smokin' hot blog, and some fun reading about some of your favorite celebrities), it's that, other than you, the single most important component of any blog are the readers. They are the Earth to your Sun. It's the perfect symbiotic relationship.

And it's important to know what they are interested in, what they like, who they want to read about, what makes them tick, how they dress, what they eat, what they do with their money, what their education levels and ages are, where they live, if they have pets, how they voted (and if they voted)—in short, basically everything you can find out about them. You can find out who they are by reading their comments, keeping an eye on which posts attract the most page views, and checking your traffic on Google Analytics, which will give you a snapshot of your blog's visitors.

Know your readers and you can write for them. Know your readers and you can target your posts to them. Know your readers and you can attract the right advertisers for them. Don't underestimate the importance of knowing who your readers are.

The core reason for writing a blog should be because you love it. Your readers should provide the fuel to keep you going. Without them, you're just standing in the middle of an interstate highway and talking to yourself: Never underestimate their role in shaping your blog, but at the same time, it's crucial to be true to yourself and who you are. It's *your* blog and it should reflect *your* interests. Use your readers' demographics to guide you to success, but never abandon your vision for what your blog should be.

That may sound contradictory—I tell you to play to your readers, but be true to yourself—but it's really not. What I mean by that is that you have to know who is reading your blog and what they expect from you, but don't box yourself in creatively. I know what my readers like and don't like, but it's still *my blog*. Sometimes I add things because it suits me. I don't monkey with the core of my blog, but if I feature an artist I like and my readers aren't crazy about, that's okay too. They don't have to like everything I do and your readers don't have to like everything you do.

Look at it this way: If you went to see Steve Harvey and he performed *Hamlet*, you'd leave the theater disappointed. You didn't go to see *Hamlet*. But if you went to see Steve Harvey and he did the show you expected plus a five-minute excerpt from *Hamlet*, you'd still leave happy. Maybe you liked that snippet of *Hamlet*, maybe not. Either way, that five minutes isn't going to change your life, but maybe it was something he felt artistically driven to do.

So be true to what your developing readership expects, but don't sell your soul.

Making money from blog posts

Posts should be moneymakers, but they shouldn't be sell-outs. You want to keep your stuff relevant, interesting, and approachable from an advertising point of view, but you want to make it known that your content isn't for sale.

Before an FTC ruling made it clear that bloggers had to properly label paid advertising and couldn't just incorporate it into a blog post and pretend it was copy, companies used to buy out bloggers. Those bloggers would post advertising in the guise of a blog post and get paid for it. Finally, the feds said that wasn't fair—advertising must be marked as advertising, just like in the print world. It's a good ruling. Without some kinds of boundaries dividing advertising and editorial, it's too easy to muddy the ethical waters. Bloggers need to have standards; not all will have the same ones, but some should be uniform and this is a good place to draw that line.

Tweeting, Facebooking, and all that jazz

Social media options keep growing, but there are only two that I think are vital to a blog's development: Twitter and Facebook. Of course, at the speed things change on the net, there could be a third big one (or one of these could fade from popularity) in the time it takes this book to go to press. But right this minute, these are the eight-hundred-pound gorillas of the social networking sites.

Most of you are probably already tweeting like crazy. If you don't have a Twitter account for your blog, you should have. Same with Facebook: Start a fan page for your blog. It's simple to set up and you should separate out the personal stuff from the fan stuff. Trust me, it will be much easier if you do this right from the beginning; mixing professional, family, and friends on social networking sites will create a nightmare you won't be able to resolve once the ball is really rolling. Even if you choose to name the blog after yourself, create those separate social networking identities. You don't want your readers (as much as you will love them) knowing the mundane details of your life. It's TMI.

Social media guru Christine Kirk says you should divide your tweeting up into four different approaches and I think she's got a really excellent approach: It's well-rounded and keeps you from appearing too self-serving. Here is the way she says you should divide your Twitter time:

One-fourth to self-promotion: After all, the whole point is to push the blog.

One-fourth to industry news: Become the go-to resource on your industry.

One-fourth to engage your audience: People like interaction.

One-fourth to contests and giveaways: They'll come back to win something.

When you post to your blog, don't forget to embed a Twitter button on each and every post. Newspapers put individual buttons on their stories so readers can easily tweet their content. Learn from them and you'll have readers steering other readers your way. That's a win-win in every book.

A last word about liability

Liability issues are so important that I want to go over the highlights of blog comments again because they're a crucial part of your overall approach to blogging.

I think comments should be moderated and that bloggers who don't moderate end up with comments sections that are a mess. Nobody wants to wade through spam bot postings, hate-filled, inappropriate speech, and off-topic posts to read the comments of others. Remember, posts can be money-makers. Advertisers will buy space on certain posts, but if they're cluttered and messy, you can inadvertently kill that potential revenue stream.

You will have to decide what to allow posters to say on your blog. I'm pretty liberal, but I keep the nasty stuff down to a minimum. I won't let comments get out of control before I step in, so moderation is key for me, and another reason I like WordPress so much. Their backend is easy.

As I have said before, I am not a lawyer, nor do I pretend to be one, so I won't tell you what you can and cannot say on your blog, or what your readers can post. My best advice if you have any questions about the legality of something that someone posted or something you want to post is to trust your instincts. If you are feeling "iffy" about it, then get an informed opinion.

I have spent a lot of time and money finding out what I can and cannot say on my blog. Even then I get plenty of letters from lawyers threatening me with legal action. It's something that you have to deal with in this business, particularly if you talk regularly about public figures, which I do.

But if you do it right, they can't and won't put you out of business.

Now on to the new.

Tackle that business plan

Before your eyes glaze over, let me acknowledge straight up that business plans aren't exactly the sexiest things going. In fact, even the idea of writing a business plan could send you looking for a few Zs. Whether you like it or not, business is exactly that: business. And you can't run one without sufficient planning.

Does a blogger need a business plan? If the blogger wants to make money, then the answer is "yes." If the blogger is simply blogging for the heck of it, then don't bother. A business plan implies that there is a cash flow. If you plan to monetize your blog, then you need one.

A business plan helps you clarify your goals, lets you weigh your options, and gives you an objective platform for measuring your success or lack thereof. And it's not a "once and done." A good business plan is fluid, a work in progress, something that you can nip, tuck, change, prune, analyze, and add to as you go along.

When should you put your business plan together? I think that's a matter of when it works for you. Some like to start off the coming year with a reevaluation of the old business plan, while others find the holidays too frantic and intense for the kind of time a business plan can take; they may do it in the middle of the year, instead. There is no right answer, but when you work with a business plan, you need to remember that it's not something you develop and then stick in a drawer. Ideally, you should pull out your business plan several times a year to see how it's going and make changes as needed. Think of it as a diet: You check its progress as you go along. If you're not happy with the direction it's taking, then you make adjustments.

Here are the elements of a standard business plan as it relates to a new blogger. (Comprehensive business plans, like the kind you would develop in order to expand your business, interest outside investment, or borrow money, are longer, more complicated, and take more skill to put together. Since you're not at that stage yet, we're going to do a "business plan lite.") I will explain how each component works into the plan as we look at the elements. I've modified the more formal model by simplifying the elements to exclude things I don't think matter when you're starting out (like the company history and an industry overview). While you might want to do a more thorough job once you're more established, this should get you started and won't waste your time:

Overview: Since you're a beginner, this is where you'll list your assets and examine where you want to head in the future.

Target Audience: Analyze your target demographic and what their needs, wants, and preferences are. This is important when it comes to determining content and attracting advertisers. Does this demographic have a lot of purchasing muscle— that's important to the type of advertisers you want to attract (and, by extension, you).

Marketing: How are you going to market to your target audience? This is a good place to take a look at all of the social media tactics you've incorporated into your blogging and the promotions you may be doing.

Competition: Analyze the competition and what they're doing. Ideally, these bloggers are blogging about the same type of content as you, and are targeting the same general group of advertisers. You should always keep up with what other bloggers are doing, especially when they are direct competitors, and a thorough analysis conducted at least once a year can help you stay ahead of the pack. If they're serious about making money, then they're going to be analyzing your blog. Repay the compliment.

Crunch the Numbers: Here's where you analyze how much it's all going to cost you and where the money will come from. For beginning bloggers, most of your early expenses will be out of pocket—at least until you can start attracting advertising. This is a good place to look at the stuff that can really run up the costs, like exceeding bandwidth or doing some advertising of your own. And now is a really great time to find solutions to expenses that could knock you flat

The key points to cover in a business plan:
An Overview
An Analysis of the Target Demographic
A Marketing Plan
A Close Look at the Competition

(remember, you can use Flickr for photos and save bandwidth problems caused by uploading them).

Keep up with what's happening in your industry

Maybe you only cover baby food—making your own, buying it, prices, trends in—but there's still plenty of industry news out there, and every once in a while, baby food makes headlines (remember the deadly formula manufactured in China?). It only makes sense to stay on top of the news that affects the topics you cover.

This is a no-brainer for me since I cover celebrities and there's always celebrity news out there. Celebrities have full-time employees whose jobs are to do nothing but keep their names in front of the public, so it's *my* job to sift through all that news and decide what's worth bringing to the attention of my readers.

Because I keep up with what's going on and who is up-and-coming, I get invitations to events I can share with my readers. Information and industry news come from many sources, and you should use them all when figuring out what keywords work for your blog.

An opportunity for creating great keywords based on personal experience came when I attended the *Essence* Music Festival and hung around backstage with Keri Hilson. I did an interview, scored some photos, and watched as she interviewed for other entertainment outlets like E. I also got a chance to see who's backstage at events like that—L. L. Cool J and Gladys Knight, anyone? Keri told us she loves Concrete Loop and that's music to my ears. Some great keywords I took away from this experience: Essence, music, festival (both singly and as an event), Keri Hilson, L. L. Cool J—the list from something like this can be long and full of opportunity.

Be open to those opportunities that will translate into traffic for your site. Celebrity sightings, especially when there are photos involved, are perfect for using as text stand-ins (thus, keywords). I made sure that photographing Keri and others at the *Essence* Music Festival upped my keyword quotient. You should too.

The show must go on

Sometimes it's not easy to do your job. History is filled with examples of courageous people who overcame many debilitating obstacles to fulfill their destinies and meet their goals. One of President Obama's personal heroes, Franklin Delano Roosevelt, suffered from polio that left him in a wheelchair and in precarious health for much of his political life. Martin Luther King worked to overcome prejudice while threats were made on his life. And performers such as Sidney Poitier, Josephine Baker, and Lena Horne broke racial barriers and cleared a path for the rest of us with their courage and talent.

I don't mean to imply that you will encounter challenges while blogging that come close to the kinds of true hardship heroes did in their lives, but minority bloggers are still fairly new to the scene and there are roadblocks you'll have to get around in order to succeed.

Of course, not all the difficulties you will encounter will be there simply because you're a minority: You will also find the simple, everyday frustrations that come with being a businessperson. There are forms to file, taxes to pay (and take my word for it, you don't want to monkey with Uncle Sam; make sure you have a good accountant to keep you honest), and tons of things that can go wrong on any given day.

Your server goes down. An advertiser fails to pay you on time. Your site is hacked. You have issues posting. A reader keeps posting hateful stuff. Spam bots keep hitting up your comments. Someone tries to rip off your brand. It happens. You'll deal with it.

One of the best and most fitting sayings about adversity comes from show business: The show must go on. You've seen the old movies where the star performs even though her heart is breaking, she's sick, or something terrible is happening in her life. Although blogging can be a little more forgiving, you are going to have to suck it up and do your work, even when you feel like there's a marching band in your head, or your favorite aunt just passed on, or your kids are home from school and won't give you so much as a minute to use the bathroom in peace, much less work on the blog.

Even when your instincts tell you to go back to bed, you're going to have to keep on keeping on. Bloggers don't have the luxury of rolling over and going back to sleep, not if they want to keep their blogs rolling.

One of my favorite people is the multitalented Estelle, who is as nice in person as she is accomplished on the stage. When I met Estelle after one of her performances, she complained that her feet were killing her and I could see why—she had on ultrahigh heels, the kind that makes your legs look like they're twelve feet long—and she had been performing in those things for two hours. Her feet were actually swollen, but nobody watching her would ever have thought there was anything the least bit wrong. She didn't let the audience know that she was in agony with every step she took.

Now, that's a pro. And that's also the way you've got to do it if your blog is going to be a success. You can't let the little things get to you, and while you might have to pause and regroup when the big things hit, there are ways to mediate their impact. Let's talk about building a team to help you over the rough spots.

The A-team

As you know, I started Concrete Loop in November of 2005, while I was still in school, and spent most of my free time working on it. After the site started building a readership, it became apparent that my free time wasn't going to stretch far enough to keep site updated as often as I hoped. That was when I started building a team to help me.

When the work and uptick in traffic became overwhelming, I went on a message board where a lot of creative types liked to hang out and posted that I was looking for a little help. Two perfect candidates stepped forward: Brian Davis and Tianna Gordon. I knew Brian was knowledgeable about music and Tianna understood fashion, so I brought them on board to take some of the burden off me. They're both awesome team players.

As the site continued to grow and move in new directions, the national political scene was really heating up. I knew that if ever there was a time to throw some politics into the mix, it was during a campaign where a black man stood a good chance of being elected president for the first time in our history. J. Dakar is a hot political blogger, and I asked him to cover election politics as part of the Concrete Loop team. He's very organized and savvy. In fact, he was the one who advised me to open a Twitter account, which brings up another point: Sometimes you need fresh ideas and viewpoints to keep things from getting stale. You can think you're on top of social media and trends, but when you're superbusy you can sometimes miss out. Having team members knowledgeable in other areas definitely makes it easier to keep your site up-to-date and gives you an edge.

You're probably wondering how you get people to help you when you don't have the budget to pay anyone. My advice is to first take a look at your followers and see if there are any volunteers for the job. You can also go to family; when I needed help at Concrete Loop, I asked my brothers if they were interested (they weren't). However, Jared, of http://JustJared.com, another Buzz Media blog, uses family members. Another way to get free help, if all else fails, is to consider an unpaid internship. You can also explore getting help by advertising at colleges and universities—even high schools, depending on the nature of your blog. If you're starting to pick up some advertising, consider paying small stipends—$50 a month—if you can't get volunteer help.

And don't forget to have a written agreement in place with your team members. Sure, they may be friends or even family, but you never know what is going to happen. If your blog blows up and becomes really big, do you want the drama that can go along with that? It's better to have it in writing, and a contract is the best thing to have, but no matter what direction you go in, you need *something* in place.

Teams trump going it alone. Team members help you strategize and give you someone to hit up for ideas and talk out issues with. I highly advise the team approach to blogging.

The Three Magic Concepts

Most of putting a blog together is hit or miss: You find a topic and a name that attracts a following and you go from there. You build your blogging business from the inside out, and if you do it the right way, you'll stand a much better chance of succeeding.

There are three magic concepts shared by all successful blogs. Make them part of your work ethic from the beginning and you'll find success that much faster. They are as follows:

Organization: Not only should you organize your content as to the order and method of posting it, but you should also look at how it fits into the entire picture.

Consistency: Your readers will grow to have certain expectations in connection with your blog. Don't let them down. They come to you because of what you've developed. If you get sloppy or off topic, they'll notice and, believe me, they'll call you on it.

Motivation: Never forget why you started blogging. Even when you're faced with tough times, don't forget where you started and where you're going. If you work hard, you'll find success.

Oh, the places you'll go

Every time I speak at a conference, someone always asks me when I'm going to write a book. Well, here you go. I put together *ConcreteLoop.com Presents: Angel's Laws for Blogging* not because I think I know everything there is to know about professional blogging, but because there's nothing out there that specifically addresses minority bloggers. I learned how to blog through trial and error. True, I started with good, basic understanding of how the Internet and computers worked, but technology changes with pantherlike speed. The stuff I taught myself as a kid is a world away from the high-speed, high-tech world we inhabit today.

My knowledge and skill levels evolved over time and yours will too. Like me, you, too, will start off with an idea, commit to making it a reality, and persevere through hard work to see it through to the end. And, like Dr. Seuss says, "Oh, the places you'll go."

I hope this book will take you part of the way there and that I've made the ride a little less bumpy.

Acknowledgments

A big thanks to Heather Chapman and the team at Skyhorse Publishing for backing and printing my first book. I hope this is the first of many.

My parents and three brothers: Garry Sr., Mamie, Garry Jr., Justin, and Jamie—thank you for always having my back and inspiring me to do my best. I also want to thank my grandmother, Shirley Spurlock, and my other family members for their support and encouragement over the years.

Carole Moore: I can't believe the book we talked about couple years ago is done. You always believed I could finish one and I will be forever grateful for all your help during this process.

CL contributors (old and new): Brian Davis, Jeffery "J. Dakar" Holley Jr., Tianna Gordon, Christine Imarenezor, and Felicia Mancini. Thank you for contributing your dopeness to Concrete Loop.

Taj Washington: You're the best photographer in the game. Keep believing in yourself and cracking those amazing jokes.

Tyler Goldman and the Buzz Media family: Thank you for believing in my vision and helping to take it to the next level.

Mr. Charles Baldwin and the team at Rountree Losee & Baldwin, L.L.P.: Best law firm in North Carolina.

Craig Bland: I will always be thankful for your support and genuine words of wisdom.

Christine Kirk: The social media guru. I appreciate the time you took out of your busy schedule to share your tips with me. I can't wait for you to write a book!

Gregory Curtis Jr.: Our late-night chats helped me clear my mind and also motivated me to keep doing my thing. Thank you.

To my many Internet friends and anyone who has given me any feedback, whether it was negative or positive. I appreciate your honesty.

Last but not least, all the Concrete Loop readers and supporters who have been there since the beginning. Thank you for showing so much love throughout the years. I hope you continue to grow with the brand and with me.

Glossary

Although you may have seen these terms defined elsewhere in this book, I wanted to give you a quick resource where you can refresh your memory. Here are some of the more important terms I've talked about here, as well as some I may not have mentioned, but are still important to know if you're going to be a serious blogger:

- Above the fold: An old newspaper term that signifies positioning of an ad or other material on the top part of the page.
- AdBrite: One of the largest and most successful advertising networks on the web, AdBrite specializes in budget options for advertisers. Web address: www.adbrite.com.
- AdGroups: African American advertising network. Sells both target-based and large ad campaigns. Web address: www.adgroups.com.
- Advertorial: Advertising that is presented as editorial. It can be on an official site owned by a company or integrated into copy on an unrelated site, as if it is a story or blog post.
- Anchor Text: Clickable text in a hyperlink. Important because the ease of click-through can affect your page views.
- Backend: The information structure or database of a website or blog. This is where posts and images are uploaded, comments edited, and style and layout choices are made.
- Bandwidth: The capacity of a blog or site to send material, usually measured in bits per second.
- Banner ad: A box with a hypertext link that, when clicked, will take the viewer to the advertiser's website. Banner ads come in differing sizes and may be animated.
- Banner exchange: An organized network that allows websites to trade banners. The network also keeps track of the number of visitors that view the ads, letting you know if the trade is working.
- Blockquote: A long quotation taken from text.
- Blog roll: List of hyperlinks used by bloggers to recommend other blogs.
- Blog wrap: See wrap-around ad.
- Blogosphere: A name for the collective of all blogs on the Internet.

- Brand: The name and identity cultivated for a product, service, or person.
- Branding: The act of establishing a brand.
- Broadband: Refers to larger bandwidth connections, such as DSL.
- Browser: A program that is used to move around the Internet and view pages.
- Cobranding: When two brands join forces and cross-promote their products.
- Contextual ads: The most common form of online advertising, these are targeted ads that match readers with their perceived interests. These ads generally draw their inspiration from whatever material is currently being viewed by the reader.
- Copyscape.com: A site that checks the content of pages against other sites for signs of plagiarism.
- Cookies: Information gathering and storage option used by sites to store preferences, purchasing information, and browsing habits, among other things.
- CPCs: Cost per click, or click-throughs. A blogger is paid based on the number of people who click on the ad.
- CPMs: Page views or impressions, measured per thousand impressions.
- Direct advertising: Independently developing, marketing, and posting ads on your blog without using an advertising company.
- Domain: A domain is a unique identifier based on the domain name system, or DNS. It identifies a blog or site on the web.
- Download: As a verb, the act of transferring data from computer to computer; as a noun, it is the information that is actually transferred.
- Extensions: This is where the .com, .net, .biz, and others come in. They all stand for different things, but the most common and most easily searched is .com, which stands for commercial. Some extensions tell visitors where they are located or what type of site or blog they are visiting. For example, .org is generally used by nonprofits and trade groups, while .co.uk is the commercial extension for the United Kingdom.
- Fair Use: The legal conditions under which you can use material that's copyrighted for free.
- FTP: File Transfer Protocol. The method used to copy files from one host to another. FTP is an integral component of blogging.
- Full ad buyout: Exactly what it sounds like—when an advertiser purchases all of the advertising on a blog.

- Google Analytics: Google's free analytical tool that lets both bloggers and advertisers see a blog's traffic statistics.
- Google AdSense: An advertising affiliate program that pays bloggers to display advertisements on their sites. The money can be very small in the beginning, but will grow with the blog. Web address: www.google.com/adsense/.
- Heading Tag: Like a headline in newspaper, this tag helps visitors better navigate your pages. Good, descriptive heading tags can pique a visitor's interest and keep them on your site.
- Hit: A request to view a page on a site.
- Home page: The main page on your site or blog or the initial page upon which your browser opens. Can also be written as home page.
- HTML: Hyper Text Markup Language. Embedded code that you use to construct web pages. One of the basic building blocks of the Internet.
- Hyperlink: A "live" link to other text. This is important because how you link to other text on your site can place you higher, or lower, in search engine placement.
- Hypertext: Any text with a built-in, clickable link.
- Internet: The connection of thousands of countless independent networks into a whole.
- Interstitial ads: Advertising that is positioned between pages.
- IP number: A computer's numeric address on the Internet.
- ISP: A business, organization, or company that facilitates access to the Internet.
- Keyword: In online advertising, keywords are words that make an article or page more searchable.
- Kontera: Cost per click (CPC) modeled advertising with in-text delivery system. Web address: www.kontera.com.
- Liability: Legal responsibility.
- Link: Hypertext that connects one photograph, page, or word to another source of information.
- Link back: Hypertext connecting to the originator.
- Login: Manner of signing onto a computer or an account. Often required in order to leave a comment on a blog or site.
- Meta Tag: Web page information that helps search engines locate that page. Your blog's "searchability" can be the difference between making real money and just getting by.
- Moderate: To preside over. Also called a mod.
- Moderator: The person who does the moderating.
- Netiquette: Good manners where they pertain to Internet use.

- Network: Connected computers with common resources.
- Open content: Data that is in the public domain or whose owner allows the public to reuse under certain conditions.
- Permalink: A link to a particular blog posting as opposed to a link to the entire site or page.
- Plagiarism: Using the work of someone else without permission.
- Plug-in: Feature enhancing software that adds to a larger piece of software.
- Podcast: Audio feed from an Internet-based host.
- Pop-ups: Ads that pop onto your screen and sometimes prevent you from clicking off a page. Common on pornography sites, they are often viral.
- Pop-unders: Ads that appear under the page and don't appear until you've shut or downsized your browser.
- Robots.txt files: A file that tells search engines not to crawl that part of your blog. Mostly used to protect information (or screen from public view unhelpful information on your blog). Remember, not everything on your blog is meant to be or needs to be searchable.
- Root page: Also known as the home page, it's usually the one with the site's highest traffic. This is the page where most of your traffic will first land—it's your readership's first impression of your work.
- Search engine: Internet-based method of searching, of which Google is the heavyweight.
- SEO: Search engine optimization. Techniques that make your blog pop up high on a search, which increases your traffic and visibility. Proper application of SEO can help increase traffic and advertising revenues.
- Tag: Both a noun and a verb. The verb means to add searchable keywords and the noun is a component of creating HTML and other computer languages.
- Takeover ads: Large, high-budget ads that are well produced and literally take over the entire screen. This ad's goal is to be entertaining enough that the viewer will want to replay it.
- Title Tag: A descriptive word that describes the content of a page. Using the right title tags can make your site more searchable.
- URL: Uniform resource locator. The World Wide Web address of a page. You can boost your visibility by using SEO principles when choosing a domain or blog name.
- Wrap-around ads: A blog post that is wrapped with advertisements. Also known as blog wrap.
- Wrapping ads: Putting a special border around ads to distinguish them from the content.